Table for One:

Essays from a Widow's Journey

Deborah Spungen

Published by
Franklyn Press
Philadelphia, PA

ISBN: 978-0692141809
Copyright © 2018 by Deborah Spungen
All rights reserved

Printed in the United States of America by CreateSpace
Bulk purchases, please contact Editor: Lisa T. Chatburn,
lisachatburn@gmail.com

ACKNOWLEDGMENTS

My late husband, Frank, always encouraged me to write another book. "Table for One" is dedicated to him with love.

In special gratitude all those who believed in me and my book:

Lisa Chatburn who spent the last year as my guide and friend; Linda Richman, my devoted reader; Dick Reda my first muse who left too soon; Bob Campbell who helped me find the words to finish the book; Chris Taylor my computer guru who put the icon "Table for One" in the middle of my home page to keep me on track.

With sincere thanks to my special friends and neighbors for their support and encouragement:

Dana Axelrod, who kept me fed with healthy food, Susan Davis my friend since we were born who checked in every day; Janet Waxman long-time friend who was writing her memoir at the same time and gave us the opportunity to compare our work; Maureen Marcus who has been planning the book party for as long as I have been writing the book; Marian Sandmaier and Daniel Sipe who introduced me to the fine art of meditation which kept me on an even keel. Tom Williams and Keith Shively who were my constant cheerleaders. For anyone I may have forgotten, please accept my apologies.

Table for One:
Essays from a Widow's Journey

Table of Contents

TABLE FOR ONE:

Essays from a Widow's Journey

"Why do you feel you have to turn everything into a story?"
　So I told her why:
　Because if I tell the story, I control the version.
　Because if I tell the story, I can make you laugh, and I
　would rather have you laugh at me than feel sorry for me.
　Because if I tell the story, it doesn't hurt as much.

(*Heartburn*, Nora Ephron, pp. 176-177)

INTRODUCTION

Eighteen months after Frank's death I headed to Florida to stay at our time-share for eight weeks of R&R otherwise called healing. I was looking forward to going as I had the year before, just six months after Frank passed away. The act of packing and getting organized seemed quite daunting, but looking back, I remembered that in years past, Frank may have not been the best partner for packing. The situation hadn't changed much as I was pretty much on my own anyway. He did pack his own things, but always waited until the night before we left which made me more than a little anxious. I could always ask him to lend me a hand which he did most agreeably so that made a difference in the packing ritual.

I looked forward to my Florida stay with mixed feelings. There was a limit to how much time I could spend exercising, reading, going to the movies, visiting the nearby mall, and sitting by the pool working on my tan and talking to friends. I needed something else to do and then a light clicked on – I would write. I hadn't written for years, at least writing for more than myself and to share with others. I had previously written and published two books, one about my daughter's murder in 1983, And I Don't Want To Live This Life and the other was a text book published in 1997, Homicide-The Hidden Victims. For ten years, I had written training programs for the U.S. Department of Justice, Office of Victims of Crime. Frank and many of my friends often asked me, "You are such a good writer, why don't you write another book?" I thought about it and often sat down at my computer with the intention of writing, but I couldn't think of anything to write about. I read a lot of fiction and considered trying that, but to no avail--the computer screen merely blinked at me.

Now I was ready. I wasn't sure what I was ready for, but I made a commitment to myself that when I got to Florida I would write for one hour every day. That may not sound like much, but I thought it was a reasonable start. I envisaged that after breakfast, checking my email, and going to down to the hotel gym, I would sit down at my computer and write—but write what?

After Frank's death, I found myself writing down various thoughts that spontaneously popped into my head. Initially, I scribbled in small notebooks that I carried with me and on scraps of paper and

2

Post-it notes stuck all over the place. I have a terrible handwriting, so I was taking a chance that all of this might be for naught as it is possible that I wouldn't be able to decipher what I had written. I had never kept a journal before and kept meaning to buy one, but never got around to it. I came into possession of a blank journal in a serendipitous way a few months after Frank died. When I was staying in Florida I had become acquainted with one of the desk clerks at the resort and we chatted occasionally. One day she handed me a little gift bag and it was a beautifully lined journal. I am not sure why she gave me such a lovely gift, as she did not know that I was writing. I accepted it graciously and immediately went up to my little apartment and started writing thoughts in it which I later incorporated into my manuscript. Working in my little time share unit was very conducive to writing. Few distractions vied for my attention. It was quiet inside and outside, and I kept my sliding door open to the Florida sunshine and breezes. There were few interruptions, and I could see the water in three directions from my balcony and hear the ocean as the waves lapped the beach.

The first day I sat down at the computer with no idea what would happen. I put my fingers on the keys and words formed themselves into cohesive sentences and began to fill whole pages. The hour was up before I had time to really think about how long I had sat there. I referred to my scraps of paper with my illegible notes and items from my new journal, but I wrote without any other compass to guide me. After my hour, I would go down to the pool where it

3

seemed all of my friends knew of my plan to write. Dick, one of the group of friends, was my self-appointed muse.

He would ask, "Did you write today?"

If I answered in the negative, Dick said, "I want you to go back up to your apartment until you put your time in."

As the days passed, I found that I was working longer and longer and without the clock to govern my writing time.

If I reported to Dick that I had written more than an hour in any given day, he replied, "You can't bank the extra time. Tomorrow you have to turn the clock back and start at one hour again."

If Dick wasn't there, other people automatically took his place, as if they were waiting in line and asked me if I had written that day. Dick even wanted me to write on weekends. We finally settled on an acceptable plan. I would write on Saturday morning, with Sunday off to go out to breakfast with friends and read the Sunday newspapers on my balcony or by the pool.

Another day when I was in Florida and was writing, I had called down to the front desk for service as I was out of paper towels. Within five minutes, there was a knock on my door and there was a house man, Benjamin, who I had met the previous week. He handed me two rolls of toilet paper, I laughed and said I needed paper towels, not toilet paper. He came back within a few minutes with the rolls of paper towels.

"Are you writing?" he asked.

When I answered in the affirmative, he responded, "I am sorry to disturb your work."

I don't know how he knew about my writing, but I would take all the cheerleaders I could get. The next day I heard a tentative knock on my door. When I opened the door, Benjamin was standing there with a copy of <u>And I Don't Want to Live This Life</u>.

"Would you autograph your book for me?" he shyly asked.

No one asked me what I was writing about or to read what I had written, it was enough for them to know that I was writing. After a month, I asked myself, "What was I writing about?" I had not planned to necessarily write a book, only to see where it took me. As the writing progressed, a "book," (dare I hope it would become a real book someday?) began to take shape. It was writing itself. Would I be writing a biography? A textbook? Fiction? A memoir? I decided to just go with the flow and see what appeared on the pages. By the time I had twenty pages written, I realized that I was writing a book, or at the very least, a guide to widowhood, and maybe some of each.

This is not a book about my husband's illness and death. Frank's death would only serve as a platform for my story. For the most part, I was writing about events that had transpired after his passing. These experiences took the form of vignettes, some short, some long, some sad, some funny. Vignettes give a person a glimpse of how life unfolds in its infinite bits and pieces. There are many ways to grieve and each person must find their own pathway. It is clear to me that my way of dealing with grief is to write about it. The perspective that the writing gave me helped me believe that my husband was indeed gone. It also gave me a focus and a goal, which is saying a lot and worth the hours I spent trying to put it all down on paper. When I became a widow, I found that defining myself solely with the "widow" word was not completely accurate because I was more than just a widow, I was still me.

I needed a descriptor that went beyond my sadness and grief. Aha, now when I wondered who I was, I could answer, "I am a writer who also happens to be a widow." That sentence rolled off my tongue without any hesitation, but now that I had committed myself to my writing, I had to do it. What I was writing was not just for me. I wasn't only externalizing my thoughts, feeling, and experiences. I wanted to share those words with other widows so that they would not think they were going through this alone while offering them a different perspective on their own experience of being widowed. This book is also intended for a wider audience of readers who are curious about how the death of a loved one resonates for all of us.

This book adds to the genre among memoirs and books written about widows, grief, and bereavement in that it is written, not only with love, but with humor as well. I took subjects that are very painful for widows and searched for the humor in them. I feel that we need to be free to laugh at ourselves and life as well. When a loved one dies, there are some people who feel that it is not appropriate to laugh ever again. Perhaps they feel that it is disrespectful to the deceased. I don't think it is possible to never laugh again. After the first hearty laugh that spontaneously escapes from between their lips these very same people are often heard to exclaim, "Boy that felt good." If you can't find anything to laugh at in life, start with watching a funny movie or TV show; that may break the log jam. If we can smile and share a laugh or two along the way, our journey through grief will be just a bit more bearable.

Along the way while I was writing this book, I shared the unfinished manuscript with perspective readers by speaking at some book and author events, perhaps just a bit prematurely in the scheme of things. I explained my process of writing as well as reading short portions of the manuscript to them. This is similar to trying out a show on the road. I wanted to see how my audience responded to my words. Did they laugh and cry when I thought they would? Did they get the essence of what I was trying to say? What didn't they understand? What more did they want to hear about?

I was surprised that quite a few attendees at these events were men. They usually came with their wives, although many of the men had previously been widowers and had remarried. The men were very articulate and asked some very perceptive questions. They were very open about their feeling and shared their own experiences of being widowed. They were quick to compare their situations with those of the widows. Several men were astonished how I was treated in interactions with entities such as credit card companies and banks, and said that those issues never came up for them. They felt they were treated differently and that it was a gender issue. The men thought that newly widowed women were often treated as second class citizens in many interactions. We had an interesting discussion about what the widowed men thought of as indignities, large or small, that widows had to tolerate and widowers didn't. They raised topics that I hadn't even considered. It had been suggested by one of the male attendees that when my book was published that married couples should read, or at least discuss, it together. There were a lot of nods of agreement from the audience on this point. Although not every couple, married or in longstanding relationships, have conversations about what would happen when one of them passed away, it is always the elephant in the room. I am not an expert on widowhood, but much of what I have written about can be used as a road map for your journey to add, delete, or incorporate with your own personal observations. We all start from the same place. It is a learning experience and we have to fill in the empty spaces.

I also shared the manuscript with some friends and acquaintances to serve as readers. The people that I asked to help me out were not what I considered close friends as I was looking for objective opinions and felt that might have been problematic if they knew Frank or me very well. The readers were not professional writers; some were retired teachers, while others were just casual acquaintances who had expressed an interest in acting as readers.

WHY WRITE A BOOK?

When I sat down at my computer in Florida and decided to try to put words to paper something I hadn't done for many years I thought I was just trying out my writing skills which were rather rusty. I had written one other book in 1983 after the murder of my oldest daughter, Nancy. That was a very different situation than the one I found myself in 2010. I had written my first book in my head prior to her death. I always knew that I would write a book about her troubled life, but did not know when. Her death was not unexpected. It was as if she suffered from a fatal disease. Mental illness and drug addiction are a lethal combination. In 1981 the rights to my book were sold to a publisher, Random House. I was given a year to complete the book, along with some financial remuneration. In 1981 there were few computers, no internet, or few cell phones. It was a lot easier for a neophyte writer like me to wall myself off from the everyday distractions of the outside world. I felt like I went to work every morning, it was my job to sit down at 10:00 a.m., write and only take a short lunch break. I also had a personal reason for writing the book. I felt that it was incumbent upon me to tell the story of Nancy's life for both myself and for all the other Nancy's and their families out there. It was a way for me to assuage all the pain, chaos, and trauma I had experienced. For me, as well as for others, writing is one way of dealing with grief. Externalizing the feelings aids the healing process, far better than internalizing the emotions and keeping them buried to burn a hole in your heart.

But why did I want to write this book? The goal was more nebulous than for my previous book. The various words, sentences, and paragraphs started to meld themselves in a more coherent whole and I began to see a book forming before my eyes. I was surprised since that was not my intent. My first book was a closed chapter in my life. But shortly after my husband passed away I started to make notes regarding how my life was in flux as my initial intent was never to write a book about him. Maybe his death would serve as a platform on which to base a new book. I jotted down whatever popped into my head that related to my new life as a widow. I wrote without a formal outline which seemed to impose itself on my thoughts as I clipped my notes together. After a few weeks I just decided to go with what I had and so a new book was launched.

This book was not just for me. Yes, I was hoping to gain a personal understanding of what I was going through and what my future might have in store for me. But the book meant more to me than just telling my personal story or that from the perspective of other widows. I hoped that widowers would find words that would resonate with them as well, in some ways the same and in some ways different. This is not simply an account of the effects on life after the death of a partner told from the perspective of a particular gender. I wanted to share what I had learned on this journey and how others could apply my story to their lives in a way that would prove meaningful. After the death of a partner the chaos that washes over us all needs to be quelled. For me, writing is the road to tomorrow.

When I went to Florida in 2011, I wrote for an hour or two a day sitting at my little wrought iron ice cream table in my apartment during the eight weeks I was there. I called it the data center as there was only one chair and the table top barely held my computer and printer. When I returned home to the Philadelphia area I continued to work. I reread the growing manuscript and edited my work fairly often. I felt that I was making good progress. I recruited friends to read the book and asked for comments which were uniformly positive. I decided to share the manuscript with my literary agent to see if it might be good enough to possibly offer for sale and publication. I was also looking for suggestions and changes that would enhance what I had written. Unfortunately, my agent was not interested and I did not receive any feedback that might strengthen the book. Although I am a person that can tolerate criticism, I was so disappointed that I put the book aside on my desk where it remained untouched for more than a year. Not writing was very painful to me for many reasons. I am a person who usually finishes what they start and I discovered, at least for now I could not complete the task that I had set out to do. My expectations were much too high based on my experience with selling my first book. It was sold without much effort, but that was a different situation. Even my computer guru would remind me when he came to make some computer repair that I had not written for more than a year. He put a big icon, for "Table For One" sitting by itself right in the middle of my computer screen to remind me of that fact every time I turned on my computer. It stared at me each and every morning when I sat down to work on other computer projects. I guess that is what is known as "writers block." I hoped that someday I would be able to complete the book. It was important to me, but I was literally stuck. Knowing that I was working on a book, many people asked me what kind of progress I was making and when it would be available for sale as a trade paperback or as an eBook. I answered truthfully that I had stopped working on it. People offered me all kinds of support and good wishes that I would be successful in finding the ability to finish. That was very comforting, but it was also a tad embarrassing.

For a variety of reasons, I decided to sell my three time shares in Florida and not to winter there anymore, at least for now. Once the sale was complete, I began to wonder what I would be doing with my time. I had some activities planned that I regularly did like volunteer work, book club, a social club, exercise, etc., but I still had a big chunk of time that I had freed up by not going to Florida. Then I had an "aha" moment. I had been handed a gift of time just as I had in previous years in Florida. I could WRITE. Making that decision was the easiest part of the activity. It took me a while to get in the groove again. I needed to get a jump start. Writing is a very solitary profession and I found it more difficult than I remembered. I decided to hire a freelance book editor, Lisa, to be my very own private cheerleader and instructor. Lisa had been working with a friend on her memoir and came highly recommended. Lisa and I seemed to have a good rapport. We met every two or three weeks and emailed if I had questions. At our first meeting we set up a schedule for me to begin my work. The first task was for me to reread the manuscript that I had already completed. I read the manuscript out loud (to myself). Reading out loud is a very effective method to fully experience the writing. It changes the dynamics of the words. I had already written more than 100 pages and the manuscript had been languishing on my desk for more than a year. I greeted it every morning with a nod and went on to other work. Now was the big reveal. I could not procrastinate any longer. I sat down and reread the book and was surprised by what I had written. It was a head start on a real book. I still couldn't seem to get to the next step which was to actually begin writing something new. Week one went by, week two flowed swiftly by and I found a lot of things to fill my days and hours, but writing was not one of them. Suddenly it was the end of the third week and still I had not written a word. Lisa was scheduled to come the next day to discuss my progress or lack of it. I was always the kind of student that did my homework as soon as I got my assignment and always handed in my assignments on time. I could wait no longer or I might as well quit. I cleared my calendar for that day and sat down at the computer and my hands began to tap out real words. I would like to tell you that there was a miracle and I finished the book that day. No, but it was almost as good. When Lisa came the next day I had something to show her and she liked my words. I was on my way. I still needed additional support so I asked friends to send me a short email whenever they had a spare moment, "Did you write today?" I promised to answer truthfully. I started to write a few hours in my day including weekends even if I only had a small slice of time available. My writing schedule was different than with my first book, but it suited my current life style and I was enjoying myself with my new found appreciation for writing again. When Frank was alive, he was very encouraging and supportive of me that I write another book, I didn't have anything to write about, but now I had something to write about and I was out of excuses. I seem to be writing a book every 30 years or so, better than not writing at all.

If asked what my goal was, I would have to say that it was to finish what I started and to have a complete book to publish and share with others. Hopefully I will have learned something about myself as well as others.

FRANK

We had been married almost 54 years when Frank died. Before I go any further, I think it is important to share some insight into our relationship. We met when I was 16 and he was 19. I remember exactly how that Friday night unfolded. It was at a place called the Hot Shoppe where teens hung out and talked and ate hamburgers and drank milkshakes. I fell in love with him that night. Frank called me the next day to invite me to be his date at a Sweet 16 party and I happily agreed to go with him and, as they say, the rest is history. He became my best friend and lover. We married very young while still in college. As many marriages do that survive and celebrate their longevity, they are a series of chapters, some good and some not so good. We travelled some difficult roads together, often as the result of the extra burden placed on us in raising our oldest daughter Nancy who suffered from a variety of emotional problems. Sometimes we were tempted to consider divorcing due to the stress that was placed on our marriage. But it was never seriously discussed. The bottom line was that we loved and cared for each other and we knew that a divorce would not change the problems we were dealing with. We also felt that we could not put the responsibility of raising Nancy onto someone else's shoulders. We would still be together handling those issues. Frank was a good guy; he was very friendly and funny, too. He was a great joke teller and adept at dialects when they were needed to tell a good joke. He graduated from the Wharton School of the University of Pennsylvania in 1957, and he started his working career as an Accountant and later a Certified Public Accountant which he never liked. Through a variety of twists and turns he found a job as a salesman in a large company that sold job lot paper (large amounts of paper that were less than perfect or damaged in some way). He would buy it and find other businesses that could use less than perfect paper. For the next 50 years the paper business was his home. Over the ensuing 50 years he worked for a few large companies and ultimately ran his own one man business and was very good at it. I was not directly involved with his business, but since our offices were often in the same space in our home I became the silent partner. When he was out of the office I answered the phone, took messages, wrote up memos, and didn't let on that I was Frank's wife. When he travelled on business I was the connection to his business. As new technologies were developed over the years, fax machines, digital cameras, smart phones, etc., it became easier for Frank to conduct his business whether he was at home or out of town. I was able to assist him as needed. At this time I was working in my own career and going to graduate school. Frank liked to discuss certain intricacies of his work and I became fairly knowledgeable of his business. When Frank was in his early 70's he had a severe heart attack and was hospitalized several times. At this time, hospitals did not allow people to use cell phones on the premises so it was difficult to work remotely. I took over as much as I could. I used to sit in the hospital cafeteria with his and my cell and keep the business going. At this time we discussed the idea of my learning the financial part of his business so, if his health worsened at some time in the future, I would be able to handle a little more of his work. We both thought this was a good idea, and I began my tutorial. His health greatly improved and Frank didn't think that he would need my assistance because he had recovered very nicely from his heart attack. He did not know what awaited him. I went along with his decision because I was not privy to the future either. I probably should have been more insistent that I learn more of the ins and outs of the financial part of the business. Unfortunately, when he was diagnosed with cancer we were not sufficiently prepared for me to take over his work. He did not have the strength to teach me. Until the last seven weeks of his life he was still working out of his small office in the lower level of our home in Water Mill, NY. He always said that all he needed was a smart phone and a computer and he was in business. By then there was not too much left to the business as he started to work less and less. Frank said, "I think I want to cut back, I will retire completely in the next few months." He didn't realize what a prophetic statement that was. He just kept a few of his good customers. From the day he was diagnosed with pancreatic cancer, he passed within seven weeks, he only went down to his desk once more during that time period. My tutorial was over. After the one visit to his office, Frank did not seem to have any further interest in his business. It was as if it didn't even exist. I was too busy caring for him, taking him to medical appointments and having him admitted to the hospitals to pay much attention to the business. Using QuickBooks, I paid the few outstanding bills and sent out some final invoices.

In the final weeks of his life Frank started to put together a bucket list, which unfortunately he was unable to complete. I think if one knows what someone's bucket list consists of, you can understand more about who they really were. Frank's top entries were getting a dog or two, (he loved our cats, but it was a dog that he really wanted) and to meet Vanna White who worked on the TV show "Wheel of Fortune." Frank loved his family very much and was very proud of his children and their successes in life. When he became a grandfather to Ella and Joey that was the icing on the cake. To say he was ecstatic was putting it mildly.

GOODBYE

The dictionary defines widow as "a woman who has outlived the man to whom she was married at the time of his death, esp., such a woman who has not remarried, the definition of widower differs only in gender –a man who has outlived the woman whom he was married at the time of her death, esp., such a man not remarried."

The definition is simple and all dictionaries offer almost the same definition. If one questions a new widow or widower they may feel that the label of widow or widower is not as simplistic as the one that the dictionary offers. Many widows, more than widowers, feel that when a person says they are a widow, there is a stigma attached to the term. The response, often unsolicited, is "I'm sorry" or some other sympathetic reply not necessarily verbal, perhaps a downcast nod or a light touch on the arm. The definition also varies from person to person, by gender, and over time as well. If a widow remarries, is she still a widow or does that role disappear? When you fill out a form at the doctor's office do you go back to checking off the "Married" box again as there is no box that states "formerly widowed or remarried?"

On July 1, 2010, I was someone's wife, I was Frank's wife. We had been married for almost 54 years. I hardly remember a life when I wasn't Frank's wife.

Exactly seven weeks prior, on a bright and sunny Friday morning in early May my husband woke up, ate breakfast, and went to the Cardiac Gym to work out as he usually did three days a week. He seemed fine when he left the house, but he came home early. I asked him, "What is wrong?" I knew something had to be amiss as he always went to the hospital cafeteria after his workout with his friends. They would sit around a big table for an hour or more, with an iced tea or a diet coke, and discuss the troubles of the world and how to solve them.

He had a variety of unusual (for him) symptoms. Frank responded, "I have pains in my hips, shortness of breath, and I feel exhausted. I don't want any lunch, I just want to go upstairs and get in my bed," where he stayed all weekend, barely venturing out for a meal. We thought that maybe it was a virus of some kind.

When a person suddenly, and with no warning, presents these symptoms, the response is not usually, "Oh my G-d, you are dying from cancer." By the next week, with an exacerbation of his symptoms and a continued terrible, pervasive exhaustion and a cough unlike anything he had ever experienced before, we started the search for an unspeakable diagnosis. This entailed going for a variety of medical tests, surgical procedures, various doctor visits, rides in ambulances, and four hospital stays in three different hospitals over the next few weeks. Still whatever they told me or whatever procedure they performed gave us no definitive answers.

21

Most doctors seem not to be able to look beyond their own paradigm, e.g., if they are cardiologists, they think the issue is heart related; if they are infectious disease specialists, they come up with whooping cough or Lyme Disease, etc.

Frank knew better than all the doctors, but they wouldn't listen to him.

"I went through a portal when I woke up that Friday morning and I can never return. I went to bed a healthy man and woke up a sick, old man," he said.

A CT Scan of his chest showed lesions in his liver, followed by a PET scan which showed a large tumor in the middle of his pancreas, followed by that awful diagnosis of pancreatic cancer. My mother had died from pancreatic cancer so we knew what the future held. There was talk about chemotherapy, but he was already too sick to physically get to the doctor for the treatments and so, his fate was sealed. Holding hands, I went through that portal with him. I did come out on the other side, but it was a different place than Frank came out. I was alone, in a different world. I was not prepared to be a widow; no one warned me of its impending arrival.

"Your husband is a very sick man," one doctor informed me, but that did not translate to me as "Your husband will die very soon, most likely within days or weeks."

My husband had a history of heart disease, but it did not greatly affect his quality of life; he exercised three times a week, even riding his bicycle five miles each way to the gym, still worked part-time, and enjoyed many other activities. If he were late coming home from the gym, I would worry that something had happened to him (I am a major worrier). Maybe he had another heart attack or some other heart related event. I never got beyond those thoughts to consider that he could die in the immediate future. I discovered that too often what you are afraid of is not the thing you need to be afraid of. I never considered that cancer would kill him, and almost as swiftly as a heart attack.

I had no preparatory course in becoming a widow; there was no handbook to read first. I knew other women who were widowed, but there were few lessons to glean from observing them except for the sadness in their eyes. I could only learn from them after I was admitted to their club. I carry some guilt that I should have done more, and said more to Frank, but I thought that we would have more time together and that he would be better soon. I think I am usually a good patient advocate, but I felt that I had been struck suddenly mute by this terrible turn of events. I sat by his side in the hospital, day after day for 10-12 hours at a time, and barely spoke to him or the doctors. All the questions I had for the doctors had disappeared from my brain. I could ask them nothing of consequence. I sat and held Frank's hand, but I had no words of solace for him; I didn't know what to say that would be helpful.

Maybe this is not really the way it happened and I had developed amnesia regarding those endless days in the hospital, but I have little or no memory of speaking to anyone or of comforting him. Family and friends find it difficult to believe that I would sit there and not speak, but that is the way I remember it. I feel I let him down and that I should have done more. I am not sure how to define "more" but maybe I could have given him a better quality of life (or of dying) or extended his life even a little bit.

While he was still in the hospital, the nurse brought him the Do Not Resuscitate (DNR) orders to sign. Frank wanted to sign the DNR. I didn't want him to do it. I didn't want his life to be over.

"Can he use an erasable pen in case he changes his mind?" I asked the nurse.

She looked at me as if I were the first person to ask such a shocking question.

His fourth hospitalization was only palliative in nature and Frank wanted to go home. Within a day's time, I turned the house into a mini hospital with all the requisite equipment, hired a nurse's aide, and he became a hospice patient. As it turned out, he was a hospice patient for only 36 hours. The social worker and nurse from hospice were coming to help guide us for what was ahead. Frank arrived home from the hospital in the afternoon and the hospice team came an hour later. They sat and talked with me for quite a while, answering my questions and providing me with information for the final part of Frank's journey which I still could not comprehend. They handed me some printed sheets about what to expect and some things to do, an instruction manual of sorts. A nurse went into Frank's room to briefly speak to him and then they left. The hospice nurse was to come back two more times the next day and then no more.

My children arrived at different times and we took turns talking to Frank and sitting by his bedside. When our daughter Suzy talked to him, he smiled at her. Our son David was at work in Manhattan and had planned to come right after work. We decided to call him to suggest he come as soon as possible, not knowing that Frank was to take such an abrupt turn for the worse. The bus ride to the Hamptons took about two hours and David joined us directly at Frank's bedside. In the morning, Frank was still telling jokes, but his condition deteriorated in the next few hours. I don't know if he could hear us, and he didn't seem to be able to communicate very much. Later as we were all sitting by his bedside, he opened his eyes again and looked like he wanted something. We offered him water, and he shook his head, "No." We went through a list of things and he kept shaking his head, "No." Finally I mentioned ice cream, his most favorite food and he smiled and nodded "Yes." And so his last meal was a few spoonfuls of vanilla ice cream which we fed him before he dozed off again. Later, I was in the room by myself for a few minutes holding his hand and I said, "I love you," and he opened his blue green eyes and started to quietly sing a few words of a song to me, "Do you love me?" and then he ran out of words and he closed his eyes. I think they were the last sounds he uttered. I cannot remember the rest of the song, only that is was from "Fiddler on the Roof."

We called the hospice nurse and she returned in about an hour. She went in to see Frank and we all stood clustered in the doorway. We watched in quiet amazement as she soothed him and ran her hands gently over his chest. It looked to us as if she were "laying hands." His face looked so calm and young.

Finally she left his bedside and came out to the hallway and spoke to us, "He is not ready to go, I could feel him pulling back, but I will return tonight." The nurse had suggested that maybe we should play some soothing music and then she left. Frank's favorite music was "The Grateful Dead," but we never got around to playing a Grateful Dead CD so his send-off was not quite as good as we had hoped.

We did not have to ask him for forgiveness for anything or say goodbye, we had already done so. We just sat quietly. The hospice nurse told us that we were to administer his morphine every two hours. Our daughter made an Excel spreadsheet and each of us were to take turns.

Hospice provides a little box containing a quantity of different medications called "The Comfort Kit." I am not sure for whose comfort it is intended, mine, his, or both of us in different ways. The hospice nurse had given me instructions on administering the pain medication. I saw how Frank was struggling to stay with me in life. I didn't think that he was ready to leave me yet. Difficult as it was, I believed that maybe I needed to let him go in peace. I whispered to him, "Good night my sweet prince, I will see you again on the other side." As I stood alone by his bedside, I administered a dose of morphine from a syringe under his tongue. I had gone upstairs to my bedroom for a moment and that is when he chose to pass away. I say "chose" because he did pick a time when none of us were by his bedside. Our children were all present in the house, but at that moment, no one was with him. Only the nurse's aide was nearby and she came upstairs to get me.

We did not know that his death was to come so quickly, just 36 hours after he came home from the hospital. I know that I will be ever haunted by the fact that I administered the last dose. I have been told by many people that it was best for Frank and that it kept him from suffering anymore, but I am not convinced.

On that early morning of July 2, 2010, the moment of transition, life slipped away from Frank and, in turn, he slipped away from me. I was told to expect that his body would be cool to the touch, but he still felt warm to me--alive. I felt his chest over his heart, but there was no heartbeat. I lowered my head to his chest and there was no discernable beat of his brave and valiant heart. I was confused by the continued warmth of his skin. I thought he must still be in there. Maybe it wasn't too late and we could do something to bring him back. I was afraid to touch him, afraid to feel his life leaking out of him as it must surely do. I did not understand that his body was just a vessel and that his soul was still with me in that room of death. But after administering the last dose of morphine, there was no turning back, it was done, his life was complete and my new journey, the one I would traverse alone, had just begun.

Initially, I felt anger towards the hospice team for putting me in such an untenable position. As time passes and I gain some perspective, I better understand why it is done that way, but it is a terrible responsibility to carry around. Yet, I felt that the hospice team made me complicit in ending Frank's life without making sure I truly understood what I had to do and getting my acquiescence to participate in the final act.

At exactly 12:45 a.m. on Friday July 2, 2010, I was nobody's wife. I was a widow. It wasn't just the abrupt loss of the love of my life, my best friend, but my status as a person was irrevocably changed in ways that I couldn't even begin to fathom. I wondered, "Who will I be if I am not the same me that I was when I woke up this morning?"

THE FOREVER GOODBYE

In the last week or so of Frank's life he was well aware that he did not have much longer to live. He was anxious to discuss his funeral arrangements with me while he still had clarity of thought and speech and he brought up the subject a number of times. One of his major concerns was where we would hold the funeral since we lived more than 100 miles from our long time home in Philadelphia. The logistics were easily resolved when I assured him that we would hold his funeral in the Philadelphia area. The other issue he wanted to discuss was the content of the service. His preference was his version of a Jewish-Quaker service in which the rabbi had minimal control over the content and served mostly to introduce the various family members to offer their individual goodbyes and to chant the appropriate Hebrew prayers. Our immediate family members – daughter Susan, son David, son-in-law Steve, daughter-in-law Aliana, and grandchildren Joey and Ella would each write their individual parts of the service and deliver it. I did not plan to speak. I made note of Frank's requests. I was having difficulty believing that this conversation was even taking place. If I had known that less than eight weeks ago someone would tell me that I would be sitting here and discussing plans for my husband's funeral with him, I would have said "You don't know what you are talking about." He seemed satisfied with those arrangements and when he passed away I followed his requests still in a state of disbelief. I was gratified that we had the opportunity to make these arrangements together as some people don't.

There were more than 100 attendees at the funeral, both relatives, business acquaintances and friends. People formed a line and slowly came up to each of our family members and greeted us with hugs, kisses and tears. The funeral went off as planned with each family member, beginning with my Joey, reading their own heartfelt words about Frank and their special relationship with him.

Frank's funeral was held on July 6, 2010. It was a hot and humid day with the temperature rising above 102, a record breaking day. Frank was born on February 7, 1934 and that day was equally record breaking with bitter cold temperatures. Frank's birth and death were bookmarked by these two distinct weather events.

WHO ARE "THEY?"

After being widowed, you hear a few basic statements that people make because they feel that they are on safe ground: #1 "Please accept my condolences" or "I am sorry for your loss." My response is "Thank you," and then the ball is in their court again. Usually that is followed by an uncomfortable pause until someone picks up the conversation by introducing another topic; #2 "How are you?" Response: "Fine, thank you" and then it pretty much picks up where #1 left off. I am often tempted to say to certain people who are in a more caring and closer relationship, "Do you really want to know?" but I am not sure it is fair to put them on the spot so I don't answer the question with a question. The other answer that I stopped using since the first year was "There are no words;" and #3 most people, including other widows, do not offer too much unsolicited advice and when they do, it is usually about "they."

Do you know who "they" are? Apparently there is a very large group of "they" around the world who make rules and regulations regarding what and when newly bereaved widows should do regarding making decisions, especially major decisions like selling your home and moving, or buying a car, or anything that seems like another major shift in the bereaved person's life. The most important advice that people feel they can offer and maybe it is the only one: "They say do not make any major decisions for the first year after your spouse has passed away." After hearing that admonition many times from many different quarters, I was considering marking the date a year hence on my calendar so I could remember it (like I didn't already know the date of the one year anniversary) when I can start making important decisions again. I thought maybe in addition to marking the date, I would start listing all the possible decisions that I would make when the year is up. I am not sure what I was supposed to do for the first year regarding major issues that needed to be addressed at the time and not postponed to a future date.

I believe that many people give that advice, which is offered in a kindly and well-meaning way, because that is what they have heard from others.   But most likely have not tested the axiom for themselves. I think what people are trying to say is that the first year after my husband's death is not a good time to make any other life changing decisions since I have just gone through a life change that was horrific and of which I had little or no control. There is a lot to be said for that line of thinking. I have noticed that regarding some decisions that I made the first year, and in looking at them in hindsight, maybe there was a better decision, but I don't think that waiting a full year would have improved my insight. Some decisions might take two or three years to make and maybe there is never one right action.

After the first few times that I was told about what "they" say, I inquired in a naive way as to who "they" were. I usually got a blank stare back which made me realize that nobody knew who "they" were or where "they" were, so I stopped asking. What would I do if I found out who "they" were? Would I try to get an audience with "they"? Would it be like going to India and climbing the mountain to a cave hidden in the mists to meet the great guru? No, I think that "they" are less anthropomorphic than that as no one seems to know where "they" live or has ever reported seeing them. It is like the search for "Big Foot" or the "Loch Ness Monster." I decided to do some research into this clan of "they" to see if I could get some more information that would help me identify 'they." I was very disappointed that I found no reference to "they" on Google or Wikipedia. I even talked to some Talmudic scholars, Buddhists and other spiritual and religious experts and no one has ever reported seeing a reference to "they" in any of the great religious or spiritual writings.

The decisions that I made the first year, some better than others, were for the most part based on my intuition and circumstances and worked for me, even though I did not always follow the advice that "they" gave me.

"They" aren't always right.

CARS DIE TOO

It was the afternoon of the first day of my life without my husband. I can almost hear what you must be thinking, Oh no, I hope she is not going to go through every single day after her husband passed away. Have no fear, that is not my plan, I want to share a few things that happened during those first few days, days like no other. The funeral home employees came to the house around 4 a.m. to take Frank home to Philadelphia for the funeral which was not until July 6 due to the July 4th holiday falling on a Sunday, making Monday, July 5th also a legal holiday. This caused some scheduling issues with the funeral home and the cemetery. Enough said about that.

My children and I spent most of the morning making all the necessary arrangements for the funeral and notifying all our family and friends of Frank's passing. My daughter-in-law Aliana drove from Brooklyn with Joey to be with us and to help. Then Susan and Aliana took me to see if I could find a suitable black dress for the funeral as my wardrobe in the Hamptons was very casual, mostly jeans and tee shirts. We took Frank's SUV and drove around to look at the few stores that might have something for me to wear. There are really no department stores in the Hamptons, except for a mini-Saks store which has since closed. Fortunately, I did find a plain black dress that would be appropriate for the widow (me) to wear to the funeral.

On the way home, we stopped for gas. When Aliana tried to start the car again, the engine was dead. This gas station just sold gas, coffee, and donuts, but not service. After a few failed attempts to start the car with jumper cables, we called a tow truck. The car was only three years old, had been serviced, and had never had any problems. The towing company came, started the car, and the driver said a light switch may have been accidentally left on and drained the battery. He assured me it should be just fine if we kept the car running for about twenty minutes. I wondered if Frank's spirit had anything to do with the car battery dying, but I dismissed that thought as being silly. When I mentioned it to my family, they just looked at me and did not say anything, and we drove home without further problems.

I was aware of what I was doing, but I felt like I was floating around on anesthesia. The day felt so surreal. One moment, I really knew that Frank had passed away, and then I felt that I was just walking through a bad dream and that he was around somewhere, just out of sight. My son, daughter-in-law, and grandson, left to go to my granddaughter at summer camp in upstate New York to bring her to Philadelphia for the funeral. Before she left for camp, Ella had said her goodbyes to her "Poppy," knowing that he was very ill and that she might never see him again. She wanted to be called at camp when Poppy died and come home for the funeral. When her parents called her, she asked if they could buy her a black dress to wear at the funeral. I am not sure where that came from, but we ended up with a dark gray and white dress, black not readily available in a nine year olds size. My daughter and son-in-law, Steve, went to their house which wasn't too far away and I was alone, but everything felt so dream-like that it really didn't matter.

The next evening, Susan and Steve had been invited to a late afternoon garden party that was more business than pleasure in nature, and they said they would only go if I went because they didn't want to leave me alone. I didn't want to go, but, as mothers are wont to do, I said I would go so they wouldn't have to "babysit" me. I didn't want to spoil their night and, again, I was feeling very disoriented. I decided to drive to their home which was on the way to the party and we would go together from there. I opted to take my car as I felt a little leery about taking the SUV after the battery had died the day before. Our other car was a five-year-old convertible which we used to drive locally, and it only had 12,000 miles. We always took good care of our cars and kept it regularly serviced. As I was driving to Susan's house, the battery light suddenly lit up on the dashboard. I rubbed my eyes in disbelief and tried not to look at it during the remainder of the ride. When I arrived, I turned off the ignition and then tried to start it again. The red light didn't come back on and the car started without a problem so I switched it off again. It was probably just an aberration and I decided that I would worry about it when we returned from the party.

We arrived at the party which was held in a very large beautiful flower garden overlooking a farm field abundant with vegetables and orchards of fruit trees approaching the peak of their growing season. It was sunny and warm and there was a lovely soft breeze blowing off the ocean. The garden's perimeter fence was punctuated by a two sided set of steps. When you climbed up the six steps and stood on the little platform you were rewarded with a spectacular view of the many acres of planted farm land sweeping down to the ocean. I took in the view and came back down. The owner was a well-known artist and it would have been special to be a guest at this spectacular property under other circumstances. I propped myself up against the railing at the side of the steps and stood there for most of the party. I felt invisible and did not try to speak to anyone. Susan and Steve brought over a few acquaintances to meet me and other than mumbling a few words in response to the introduction as I wasn't capable of carrying on a conversation. I looked at my watch realizing that it was only 36 hours since Frank had died. I tried to fathom why I was standing in the middle of a beautiful garden by myself on a lovely Saturday afternoon. It felt like an out-of-body experience.

When the party was over I drove back to Susan's and got in my car and headed home. I held my breath, but the car started without a problem and I drove out onto the road. At first I thought that I was imagining the car was moving slowly, but then I realized that it was not my imagination--the car had really started to go slower and slower so I pressed harder on the gas pedal and the car went even slower--the next step was the slowest of all—a dead stop. Talk about feeling powerless—I was in the same state as the car. I felt like I was in a car without a driver. I almost made it to the intersection where there was a small market. I made the turn and glided to a dead stop in the middle of a two lane country road which was crowded with cars and bikes and people going in and out of the market to buy coffee, snacks, newspapers, and picnic lunches to take to the beach. There I was sitting in a car in the middle of the road and no one paid any attention to me--they just walked around.

I was invisible and apparently my car was, too. I called Susan and Steve and they said they would be right over. While I was waiting, a nice looking gray haired gentleman, dressed in the Hampton summer uniform - bathing trunks and a tee-shirt advertising some kind of 10K race and flip flop sandals - came up to my car, looked in the window at me sitting in the middle of the road with a confused look on my face.

"Are you OK? Is something wrong?"

Instead of simply saying, "Could you please help me, my car broke down." The answer that he got from me was the whole story in one breath.

"My husband died yesterday and his car broke down yesterday and it was a battery problem and today I took my other car and the same thing is happening today and my car is stuck in the middle of the road. I called my daughter and AAA towing service, but no one has come, yet."

After that, the man immediately jumped into action. He authoritatively called over two young men who were walking around my car as if cars were always parked in the middle of the road and strongly invited them to come over and help. They didn't look thrilled, but they obeyed. The gentleman looked like he was used to being in charge and having his instructions followed. The three of them pushed my car, while I steered, to the side of the road where there was parallel parking. The young men took off without even waiting for a "thank you." I guess they were afraid that they might be called upon to do repair work on the car. I thanked the man.

"Are you OK to wait alone for the tow truck?" he asked.

At that moment, my daughter and son-in-law drove up and then the man took off. I nominated him to be my fairy godfather for that day. Susan and I sat on a small wicker love seat under a large sun umbrella in front of the market to wait for the tow truck. We just sat there watching the constant stream of people coming and going in and out of the little market, laughing, smiling, and talking to each other, a perfect summer day. I felt like I was in another orbit – like one of those weird science fiction programs on TV and I didn't belong in their world anymore. These people were living their lives just as they did the day before and the day before that.

I wanted to say, "My husband died yesterday and I am not in your universe any more. Can't you see that? How can you be walking around and having a good time just like you were yesterday?" But I knew it would be fruitless if I tried to say that because no words would come out of my mouth and if they did, no one would hear or notice my pain.

"I think your Dad is so powerful that he is still here and is making sure that we know it," I said to Susan.

"Mom, yesterday when you said you thought it might be Daddy's spirit that spooked the car, I thought maybe you were just making a bad joke. But today when your car died the same way, I am starting to believe that Daddy had something to do with it."

"There are no coincidences," I replied.

It took more than an hour for the tow truck to come. It was the same tow truck and driver that had responded the day before. The driver looked at me and asked,

"Aren't you the same woman from yesterday? The one whose husband just died? What is your husband doing to your cars?" Maybe he had seen this before.

He said it seriously, too. He worked on the car for a while and it wouldn't start.

"What's wrong with it?" I asked.

"It is not the battery, I think it is the alternator and I will have to tow it. Do you want me to tow it to the dealer?" he asked.

I noticed that the AAA paper work said that if the car cannot be driven, the tow company will take it to your car dealer or a service garage, but they cannot do that unless you ride in the cab of the tow truck with the driver. After the tow truck drops you and the car off at the dealer you have to arrange your own transportation home. It was Sunday and the dealer was closed and closed the next day, Monday, as well. I was leaving very early on Monday morning for Philadelphia to make the arrangements for Frank's funeral and to attend the funeral on Tuesday. I wouldn't be back for a few days.

The driver looked at me and said, "If you give me the owner's card, your car insurance and contact information, I will take your car to the dealer."

"Don't I have to go with you?" He looked at me and shook his head.

"No, you don't need to do that; you have been through enough already. I'll deliver the car to the dealer for you and put the paper work in the service slot. Boy, I don't know how both of your cars died in the first two days after your husband died."

Susan and I just looked at each other. It seemed kind of strange to us, too. Susan and Steve drove me home. The more I thought about the car issues, the more I believed that something other worldly was going on. I don't believe in ghosts, although some people I have talked to feel their loved ones presence in the room, but may not actually see them. This seems to appear more often to young children whose parent has died. But what I was experiencing was not in the same realm. I have read that people see someone walking down the street and they think it looks like their deceased loved one, but if they call out their name or run up to the person, it isn't them. There may have been some resemblance, such as the way they wear their hair or the way they walked or even an article of clothing they were wearing like a baseball hat. But this is not the same as seeing a ghost, it is more like a Gestalt (when the experience is considered as a whole and regarded as amounting to more than the sum of its parts).

What I was experiencing seems fairly common. Sometimes it is just a feeling that you can't shake--sometimes there is an event, such as with the cars, which feels like strong evidence that the deceased is still present. This seems to occur more in the early weeks and days closer to the time of death, but for others it may persist for years. Many, including me, are not frightened by such experiences, but rather welcome them. It can be quite comforting to believe that your loved one is still near. You may not believe in the veracity of these occurrences. I think that it depends on how tuned in people are to the spiritual world in the early days after the death. Some people have a sixth sense in these matters. I think everyone does, but some people are more aware of it.

You may think that the two incidents with the car were nothing more than a strange coincidence, but I don't buy into that. As time moves on, I have had more instances which for me, made it quite clear that Frank was still nearby. I had set a timer on the lamp in my living room to go on in the early evening. I noticed that it had stopped working. Taking care of making sure the light worked properly was one of the recurring jobs that Frank had on his "honey do list." I didn't put this in the category of brain surgery, so I decided to give it a try. I opted to put a new light bulb in the lamp first, but that didn't make any difference. I got down on my knees and started twirling the time dials to read approximately 8:00 p.m. for the light to go on and 2:00 a.m. for it to go off. The real test as to whether my work could be considered successful would be when it got dark. I began by checking the lamp at dusk, nothing. An hour later and still nothing. I checked the dial and it seemed correct. I gave up after that and didn't bother working on it any further. I relegated it to the "not very important" list and promptly put it out of my mind. Three weeks later, I was eating dinner in the dining room and I heard a loud click coming from my living room. The room suddenly was suffused with the light from the lamp. That seemed rather mysterious as no one else had been in the house. I walked over to the lamp and bent down to get a better view of the timer dial which was in a different position than when I was trying to set it. The next morning when I awoke, I saw that the light was no longer on. The next night the light again performed as it should, both turning off and on at the correct times as set on the dial. I scratched my head in amazement, but I shouldn't have been really all that surprised; the light continued to operate properly until I moved.

I went to my Widows Support Group that afternoon and told the living room light and timer story and none of them seemed to be that astonished. They all agreed that it was Frank's handiwork. This opened the door to the telling of similar other stories that had occurred to them as well and made them feel the continuing presence of their husbands. Barbara said, "I am reluctant to discuss these events with other people, including my children because they might think I am crazy. We all shook our heads in agreement and as one of the sisterhood concluded, "We honestly don't think we are crazy. We are just letting ourselves be open to the universe and allowing our strong men to make their presence known."

I was walking to the bathroom to shower, a few months after Frank's death, and noticed a wooden toothpick on the floor. I bent down to pick it up and look at it. Frank always had a toothpick, just like this one, handy in the console of his car or in his pocket. I, on the other hand, never used a toothpick. How did this one get on the floor? It was not there when I went to bed the night before. The errant toothpicks continue to appear in strange places and times such as in the console of my car that I bought after Frank died and in a ceramic dish in my friend's guest bedroom where I was staying. I did not see an unexplained toothpick for almost a year. It made me feel sad, as if he had really gone away this time. Yesterday as I was typing this section of the manuscript, I opened my apartment door and walked out into the hallway and there was a toothpick on the carpet in front of my door. I smiled and stepped over it and continued on my way to the elevator.

"A PROPER DINNER"

Most people have rituals around eating. They incorporate these rituals when they eat together with family and friends regardless of which meal it may be, including holiday meals. One of the first difficulties in establishing this new life as a widow has to do with mealtime. I had no idea that it would be fraught with such complications. I have been eating and preparing meals all of my adult life without any major issues. Who knew that when you become a widow all the rules for preparing and eating meals are out the window? I didn't pay much attention to the rituals until they were suddenly erased.

Over the years I have eaten with my husband and/or children, eaten by myself, and other permutations, but this dinner was special, because it wasn't just that I was eating alone, it was to be the first of many meals alone, maybe eating alone the rest of my life and it was not by choice. I felt that there was a new protocol that involved eating and I didn't know the rules. No wonder many new widows either eat too much or not enough, because they don't know the new rules for eating either. These rules should be included in a section of The New Widow's Guidebook (not yet written).

Most people, family, friends, and acquaintances really don't know what to say or do with you. They live in fear that anything they do will make you, heaven forbid, cry so they handle you with kid gloves and go for the safe things to talk about. One of those neutral conversation items has to do with eating. After all, everyone has to eat sooner or later, don't they? Many people asked me not just whether I was eating, but what I was eating. This question showed concern by others for my well-being and my answers were fairly limited and monosyllabic, e.g., "Yes," "No," or "Sometimes." I would occasionally mention healthy foods, and that seemed to please them. I would keep the verbal interchange short so as not to further upset me or them. I was admonished to eat three proper meals (what is a "proper" meal?) a day like I was a child. Rather than offering me good nutrition hints, it would have been more appreciated to have someone bring me a cooked meal. This is an area were widowers are often treated differently than widows. Men seem to get home cooked meals brought to them much more often than widows do.

During the seven weeks of my husband's illness, I had not been able to eat my meals on a regular schedule or seated at a table. If I had been eating at all, I was sitting on an uncomfortable chair by his bedside, at home, or in the hospital or I often ate standing up because, if I was home, I was multi-tasking. I might also be making phone calls or paying bills. My "meals" might consist of all or any of the following, a pretzel, a piece of cheese, a hardboiled egg, or a ½ peanut butter and jelly sandwich. I had no appetite for anything else. In the hospital I ate all my food by 11 a.m. which my loving daughter had packed for me to take in a little insulated bag, like my children used to take to school. Once or twice I went out to a late dinner in a restaurant with my daughter after hospital visiting hours. I ate like this until his death, then other things needed my attention; there was no time to shop, prepare, or an appetite to eat a "proper" meal.

One couple invited me to come to their nearby home to share dinner with them on a weekly basis. Carolyn was a fine cook, so I knew that once a week, I would enjoy an excellent dinner with friends. I could elect to talk or not talk, and talking about Frank was quite acceptable. After dinner, they immediately released me to go home, walking me to my car for the short drive. It was more for sustenance than a social outing. Two weeks after Frank died, another couple invited me to dinner. I thought it would "be good" for me to get out, but they had invited other guests that I did not know. In hindsight, it was not a good idea for me to go. I am sure that the hosts only meant well, but hadn't really thought this through. Obviously the guests had been forewarned of my husband's recent death so that they wouldn't say anything inappropriate to me. That was an awful experience, I was so shocked I had little or nothing to add to the conversation (unlike my usual loquacious self). I felt invisible as if they were looking right through me, like I was wrapped in cellophane. If I mentioned my husband's name in some appropriate context, for example, in a discussion of travel, everyone averted looking at me and changed the subject. It was like I had stunned them by using profanity. It was better to be silent, which took less effort than talking and being concerned that I would say the wrong thing and make them even more uncomfortable. The next week a couple, with whom we had been quite friendly, asked me to join them at a restaurant. That seemed like a welcome interlude. However, they refused to go to a restaurant where we all used to dine before my husband got sick, as they felt it would be too difficult to eat there as it would remind *them* too much of Frank.

I *thought*, "Whose husband died?" I never quite got this idea that my needs had become less important to them than my husband's were (and he had passed away!). It was as if I had never been part of the friendship. There weren't too many friends that excluded me after Frank's death, but some clearly moved away from me. Other widows report that it is fairly common that friends, especially couples, disappear after the death of one's spouse. This seems to be one more example of a gender issue as widowers seem to be included more in social activities than widows. When I spoke to our doctor a few days after Frank's death, he warned me that this was a common occurrence and to be expected. I wondered what he was talking about – Not my friends! I found it quite surprising, as if I were somehow contagious, but they never let me out of quarantine and the relationship was over without a word or explanation. It was another loss for me to process.

CHARGE IT!

Since most of the other dining alternatives had not worked very well, I began to think that the best bet was to try to eat dinner at home alone. Six days after Frank had passed away, I had gone to a large local gourmet market to buy some prepared foods that I could just pop in the microwave and eat for dinner. I did not have the energy or focus to cook. I wasn't really very hungry. I was beginning to take the admonishments of others seriously and thought I should try to eat a real meal. This was not as easy as it seemed. Many barriers stood in my way to getting to my goal of eating dinner home alone.

After I made my choices, I proceeded to the checkout counter where a digital cash register with a large computer screen was positioned at an angle so that the cashier and the customer could see the screen at the same time. I handed the cashier my American Express card. I wasn't paying attention to the screen when I heard the cashier's voice break into my reverie (which is where I was usually hiding out).

"Your card was denied," she said.

It seemed to me that the word, "DENIED" was suddenly emblazoned across the screen in large capital letters like on a movie marquee. I was sure that the display was big enough for everyone in the store to see clearly.

I responded, "It must be a mistake, please try it again."

"DENIED" popped up a second time. It seemed to me that the letters looked even bigger than the last time. I was surprised since I knew that I had recently paid the bill in full. I reached into my wallet and took out a different American Express card for another account. I thought, "This one will surely work." You guessed it, but this time the word "DENIED" seemed even brighter. My face felt hot and flushed. I knew I was in trouble. I meekly paid $16.43 in cash and headed home. I did have a cell phone, but I wanted to go home so I could check my records, then call American Express, and hope I had a fighting chance of not having my call disconnected. Maybe Frank had taken his card with him to wherever he was, was charging things, and he had maxed out the card. Having such thoughts was evidence of the emotional state I was in. I was so upset that I could hardly see to drive, my heart was beating rapidly, my mouth felt dry, and I was short of breath. Fortunately I lived less than 10 minutes away from the store. I took a deep breath and exhaled (the exhale is as important as the inhale), and got my paper work and called American Express Customer Service.

When the customer service representative answered, "Mrs. Spungen, please accept my condolences on the death of your husband," I knew I was in deep trouble. I wondered "How did this stranger know of my husband's death? Was she a long lost friend or relative? Had American Express, as a new service for its long-time customers, sent

51

her to attend the funeral?" I know that American Express had not sent a condolence card or flowers.

I asked the customer service representative, "How did you know that my husband has passed away?"

"Social Security notified us."

I thought that unlikely due to the privacy laws that Social Security is supposed to have in place. I jotted this fact down on a piece of paper so that I could verify the information along with the customer service's representative's name. My lawyer did contact Social Security the next day and did indeed substantiate that Social Security does not give out that kind of private information. To this day, the mystery of how American Express knew about Frank's death so quickly has never been solved. I have heard rumors that there is some kind of secret computer program that American Express uses to compile death notices and match them with cardholders accounts.
I asked, "Why were my credit cards denied?"

The agent replied, "We sent a letter to you about this, didn't you get it?

The answer is, "NO" and to this day, this letter has yet to arrive.

The customer service representative continued, "You are not the primary card holder (even thought I had had the card for many years), but you are the secondary card holder and you have no American Express cards solely in your own name."

Years before, when I was working, I did have my own card in which I was the only card holder, but I had cancelled the card after I retired thinking that the extra card was redundant. Wrong! I mistakenly thought that since we both had cards that were billed together, we were equal signers on the card. Most married women I talk to believed that this is the way the cards work, too.

Not only did I not have a husband anymore, but my widowhood relegated me to having no credit cards either. After an hour on the phone and being passed from various departments in the American Express labyrinth, I was told that based on a number of factors (not clear what they were), I was to be issued a new credit card in my name and they would be sent by overnight mail to me. I did have the replacement cards the next day as promised. I think that American Express should reconsider how it handles this issue with new widows and that couples who share a credit card need to be made more aware that they aren't really sharing it. Even my attorney did not make me aware of this issue. Visa did the same thing, but it took them a month to contact me. Perhaps their secret computer program was not as thorough as the one American Express uses. The Visa representative was very unpleasant. She informed me, with an incredible nonchalance, "Your credit card will be cancelled within 10 days and, if you want to charge anything, you better do it quickly." No matter what I said, she insisted that there was nothing that I could do to change their decision, except re-apply as a new card holder. Later that same day, I related the Visa phone call to my son, David.

"They can't do that. Call back and ask to speak to a supervisor," he said and I did.

I sighed in frustration before I spoke to the supervisor, having no confidence that I would achieve any acceptable solution. Once more I explained my situation. Much to my surprise, the supervisor treated me with a kind and pleasant demeanor and she wanted to be helpful in resolving my situation. It took her about 45 minutes, most of the time, I was just holding the phone and waiting for her to come back on the line. But she kept coming back to me and informing me of every step she was taking and how long it would take.

"What is your home number in case we get accidently disconnected? I promise to call you back so you won't have to tell someone else the whole story again."

When she got back on the phone line, she said, "I have it all worked out, your card will not be cancelled, and you will have the same credit limit as before. It will take them until tomorrow to make the name change and do the necessary paperwork. As soon as the changes are complete, I promise I will, personally, call you back."

How refreshing it was to find someone who knew how to do their job and wasn't challenging me by making me feel that I had done something wrong. It got even better. She called back at 5:00 p.m. that same night, less than two hours later,

"It is a done deal and everything is in order."

I am sorry that I never wrote down her name so I could let her supervisor know what an outstanding job she had done.

The next day I went to Brooklyn to visit my family for a few days. My then nine-year-old granddaughter Ella, showed me a letter that she had gotten in the mail that day. It was from one of the major credit card companies with a plastic credit card affixed to it. The card was co-sponsored by one of the airlines. My granddaughter travels with her parents quite a bit on vacations and she is enrolled in the Frequent Flyer programs of a number of airlines. The letter offered her a credit card through this alliance and all she had to do was sign the agreement and mail it back or call an "800" number and the credit card would be activated. As a bonus, the first time she used the card, 10,000 Frequent Flyer points would be automatically deposited into her Frequent Flyer Program. Of course, Ella was perfectly happy to remove the card from the letter and put it into her wallet and pretend that it was real. I, on the other hand, was flabbergasted as I thought, "How could a nine-year-old who doesn't even have a job be offered a credit card and I have mine cancelled because my husband passed away after being a good customer for more than 45 years? What's wrong with this picture?"

TABLE FOR ONE—PART 1

After I finished dealing with American Express, I hung up the phone and realized that I had never put my food in the refrigerator. It was probably spoiled anyway and I was too exhausted to eat. I didn't think that I would ever get to eat the dinner I didn't want, and I didn't really care. Besides it was only 5 o'clock. If I ate now, I would feel that it was the early bird special. By 7 p.m., I was feeling a bit less exhausted, a little hungry, and I had nothing else to do so I decided to give dinner a try. Over the next few weeks, the actual dinner time proved elusive, too early left me with a long lonely evening and too late proved to be almost my bedtime.

I opened all the little containers, almost like Chinese take-out, put the food on a plate, and heated it in the microwave. I took my dinner over to the dining table and sat down. I was seated in my chair and facing Frank's empty chair. That was too awful to handle so my next step was to establish a new seating protocol. What had been a table for eight, had morphed into a table for one, but it was the same table surrounded by eight chairs, of which seven chairs had now become redundant. The following night I tried sitting in Frank's seat facing my empty chair. That was just OK, but I was still uncomfortable. I had a beautiful screened-in eating porch with a view of the flowers and trees, so if the weather cooperated, I would eat my meals out there and that was calming and peaceful. As the weather turned from July to August to September and got cooler, I was forced indoors to eat my meals. I tried eating in front of the TV, but the coffee table was too low to sit comfortably and eat. I went to KMart and bought a really inexpensive ($12.99) and ugly TV tray table. I never owned a TV table before and wasn't sure how to choose one, so I went for one that was easy to open and close, seemed strong enough to hold a plate and a glass, and was cheap. I plunked it down in front of the TV, got my *New York Times*, and ate my meals at my new table for one in front of the TV.

The first time that I ate on my little tray table, my face was wet with tears. I had never eaten on a TV table before, and I pictured myself eating alone like this in front of the TV for the rest of my life. I thought the next step might be eating TV dinners, I felt that I had joined a monastery as a monk who had been relegated to eating silent meals at a table for one. I hadn't realized that widowhood sentenced one to such a punishing, deafening silence, especially at mealtimes.

I guess you could say that I was multi-tasking, eating, reading the newspaper, and watching TV and that I should have only focused on eating, but I just couldn't do it. Even when my husband was well, we read the newspapers while eating breakfast. Frank was a big sports fan. At breakfast he thoroughly read the sports section before he read anything else. Once I got my new eating arrangements relatively settled, I noticed a strange turn of events. I guess you could say that I had always been a sports fan, but not a rabid one like Frank. I could take it or leave it, but I often kept him company while he watched games on TV and I read the paper or a book. I suddenly seemed to have become a dedicated sports fan, especially of the Philadelphia teams. I started my day by reading the sports section of the paper as I ate breakfast. I don't recall ever reading the sports section with more than a glancing interest before. I discovered that many of the regular sports columnists were excellent writers and found their columns very compelling to read. When I did return to live in Philadelphia that spring, my evening or weekend was not complete if I didn't watch the Phillies on TV. It was as if Frank had channeled his love of all thing sports into me. I found I could discourse on the finer points of the games and the statistics with male friends and my grandson (which duly impressed him). I seemed to have taken Frank's place and have gotten a new hobby, being a sports fan. I also watched "Jeopardy" during dinner, which Frank and I always did together, but he was the expert. Many years ago, he had even tried out, unsuccessfully, to get on the show. I knew some answers, but my knowledge of trivia was far less than his. I realized while eating dinner by myself and watching "Jeopardy" that I was calling out the correct answers to Alex Trebek, the host of the show, more and more frequently than before. I guess Frank had also channeled his "Jeopardy" expertise to me, too.

Eating in a restaurant with friends, especially married couples, has its own set of issues beyond my always feeling like the "odd man (or woman) out." Who pays for my dinner? I never thought that being widowed gives you a free pass for meals consumed in a restaurant. Widowhood does not come with a book of tickets for complimentary dinners. I expected to pay for my own dinner. The first time I ate with another couple, when the check came, I took out my wallet and my credit card and my friend's spouse, waved it off and paid for my dinner, no matter how I protested. I said,

"Thank you, but only this time."

This little scenario repeats itself fairly often and some friends continue to treat me and some don't. The only way to avoid it is to speak to the wait person before you are seated and tell them to give you a separate check, but I often forgot to do this as this was a new way of doing things for me. For more than 50 years I never had to think about who pays the check. One time I forgot to mention the check to the waiter and I was admonished by someone at our table that I really needed to remember to tell the waiter before I was seated. It made me feel that I was trying to get a free meal. I think I have handled this issue by writing the following words with a magic marker in the palm of my left hand, "separate checks" like people used to do in high school as a form of cheating, called a "pony." This seems to work, but then I can't wash off the words on my hands for a few days or if I use a washable marker and get the palm of my hand wet, like when I am holding a glass of water, then I end up with marker on my face or an ink smeared palm. After some time went by, I began to remember to tell the waiter. For every change in my life, it is never simple and I have to work through it.

LOST AND FOUND: A SENSE OF HUMOR

My family and I held a memorial service for Frank one month after his death at the Library of the Hamptons in Bridghampton, New York where we were living and where we both volunteered. The funeral was held in Philadelphia, so many of our local friends were unable to attend. I was co-president of the Friends of the Library and Frank had served as a bartender for the Fridays at Five weekly summer program, so I thought this was a perfect place to hold the event. The community room had glass walls overlooking a beautiful garden.

We had already said all the very sad words at Frank's funeral, so this was an opportunity to say some things about Frank's life that many friends did not know since we had only lived there for the past ten years. I spoke about Frank, and his bigger than life personality that made him everyone's friend, and his bucket list which included a dog or two--and to meet Vanna White, co-host of Wheel of Fortune. My daughter made a six minute video on her Apple computer accompanied by the Grateful Dead song, "He's Gone Now." He was a big fan of the Dead, if not quite "A Dead Head." Susan looked through our boxes of old photos and did a retrospective of his life from a small boy to Susan's wedding to Steve three years before. My daughter-in-law wrote and sang a song parody to "Guys and Dolls." And lastly, David had combed the Internet for Jewish jokes to tell. These were not among Frank's personal repertoire (he was a wonderful raconteur equipped with a variety of ethnic accents), and David explained, "These are jokes my father wished he knew."

Other people got up and told some stories about Frank, some sad, some funny and some bittersweet. One of the speakers was Jason, the owner of a local coffee shop that Frank frequented on a daily basis. He appreciated Frank's humor and his loyalty as a customer. His memorial to Frank was that he named Frank's favorite coffee blend after him, "Frank's French Roast" and he had signs printed up to be placed permanently on the coffee urn for as long as he would own the coffee shop. The memorial service was scheduled for 2 p.m. on a Sunday. I had asked Jason to cater the reception with coffee, fresh baked cookies and brownies, and he would not accept any payment in appreciation of Frank's patronage and friendship.

Being the ever-present Jewish mother, I was concerned that there might not be enough food for the 75 people gathered there and I went to the supermarket and bought a variety of cheese and crackers and big bunches of green and purple grapes. I arranged the grapes in a large stainless steel bowl covered tightly with big sheets of silver foil so the grapes wouldn't spill out in my car trunk as I drove to the library. After the service was over, my family and I prepared to leave. A number of my children's friends from out of town had come to the Memorial Service and they all decided to go back to Susan and Steve's house to have some more time together. I walked alone to my car. I noticed that when I got to the car, I was about to enter it from the passenger side, half expecting Frank to be getting in the driver's seat, but I caught myself and walked around to the other side of the car. No one asked me if I was all right to go home alone, but I looked OK (no one had noticed that little slip-up when I was opening the wrong car door). I didn't say that I wasn't really OK and feeling emotionally overwhelmed by the service. I am sure my children were feeling a sadness as well and mothers like to spare their children from further pain. My children packed up the leftovers and put them in my car trunk and we all drove off in different directions.

My drive home took only about five minutes. I opened my trunk to take out whatever had been loaded in there and I gasped. Thinking that either the grapes had all been eaten or the remaining ones had been thrown out, I was surprised to see that a lot of grapes remained—I had bought a lot. In the five minutes of driving, they had all spilled out of the bowl, as the silver foil had not been replaced. Many of the grapes had become loosened from their bunches. All these single grapes were rolling all over the trunk. At the time, I had a sedan with a very large trunk which is convenient for luggage and packages, but not loose grapes. I reached to pick up the grapes, which somehow seemed to have increased exponentially in number and settled toward the back of the trunk. Try as hard as I could, I could not reach them. I tried to figure out a way to retrieve the grapes. Leaving them in the car trunk was not an option because eventually they would rot.

I went into the house to get my "grabber" (a long handled device with a hook on the end for grabbing items that people with certain disabilities can't easily do). I used the grabber to reach in the trunk and grabbed a grape. It squished. What did I expect? I attempted one more "grab," with a more gentle touch, but to no avail. At this point, I was starting to feel sorry for myself, as well as sadder, and angrier. I am not sure who the anger was directed to, maybe towards Frank, my children, myself, or to a greater spiritual being? I had another idea. I went back into the house and got a small step stool and carried it out to the open trunk, put my cell phone in my pocket (more about this later), climbed into the trunk and crawled to the back. I have read of people who were locked in a car trunk, accidently or on purpose, and I immediately thought, "What would happen if the trunk lid fell and locked me in there?" I did remember that automobiles manufactured after a certain recent date, were required to have some sort of release built into the trunk that enabled anyone locked in there to open it from the inside.

My car was brand new so I guess I lucked out on that score. There was a big yellow handle hanging from the inside of the trunk lid, which I assumed would do the job. That did not totally assuage my fears, (you have to consider the state I was in by that time) so I made sure that my cell phone was handy. I proceeded to painstakingly pick up the grapes, one by one. I was thinking that if I stomped on them to make wine, it might have been easier and more fun. As I finished divesting my car trunk of grapes, I started to think what if someone had driven up my driveway and saw me in the trunk of the car surrounded by grapes, tears streaming down my face and muttering to myself. The very thought of such an outlandish picture made me laugh, my first good laugh in a month, and every time I think of that sight I laugh again. I covet the funny memories as I moved along in my journey. I am not sure if I am laughing at myself or the circumstances that I have created, but either way a laugh is a laugh and lights my way through the tears.

My sense of humor has always been an important part of who I am, but after Frank passed away, I thought I had lost my ability to laugh at myself or at the world. Now I know that the laughter was buried somewhere deep inside of me under all the grief and pain, but I also now recognized that my sense of humor was still alive and well and just biding its time to bubble up to the surface again when I least expected it.

Slowly, over the course of a year, my sense of humor began to spontaneously return. Laughing out loud is very healing and having other people join you in laughter feels good, too. Many people feel that if a loved one has died, it is not appropriate to laugh while you are grieving, but that is not true. The line between laughing and crying is very thin. Laughing can be as healing as tears and sometimes one can morph into the other at the blink of an eye. On the other hand, it is important to consider if the laughter and re-emergent sense of humor isn't a way of burying the pain. Humor can also be used as a blanket to cover up the sadness and pain inside. I have wondered, "Am I doing that?" I don't think it really matters, laughter makes you breathe and makes everyone around you feel better.

I have noticed lately that my sense of humor is more than intact, perhaps it has even been heightened by my new life. Sometimes it seems that I go out of my way to find the humor in situations and to make others laugh. My humor often tends toward the cynical and even if something on the surface doesn't seem too humorous, I can usually dig until I find that aspect in almost any situation. If you can laugh at yourself and at circumstances that befall you in life this can be useful in accepting life's situations. Some people say that I have a "dry" sense of humor and they enjoy it. I was recently asked by an acquaintance if my sense of humor was genetic. I didn't quite know how to answer that question, I often feel like I am in the running for the "Funniest" title for the high school yearbook or trying out for a spot in a comedy club. People may make note of the humorous aspect of my personality and then they think I must really be OK. If I can leave people laughing, even strangers on the phone, I feel like I have been successful and it makes me feel better. I had discovered a yoga class, called "Laughter Yoga," which I renamed "HaHa Yoga." If you forget how to laugh, this is the place to go to find your laugh. First you fake the laugh and before long you are really laughing out loud at yourself or with the other people in the class. Laughing out loud is similar to yoga breathing and clears your head. HaHa Yoga is a wonderful antidote to depression and anxiety. For me, it was another step in reconnecting to my sense of humor.

HOME SWEET HOME

I didn't feel safe anywhere in the world, after the death of my husband. Not the kind of safety having to do with things like crime or accidents, but more the lack of an emotional safety net. Whenever I left my home for any reason, such as to do errands, go to the doctor, or to the store, I could not wait to go home again. Sometimes I would return home without accomplishing what I set out to do because I just needed to get home. I was afraid I would get lost and not be able to find my way home, like Dorothy in the Wizard of Oz, and I didn't have a pair of magical ruby red slippers to click. During the first months after Frank's death, if I went out to meet with friends or go shopping, after a short time, I would become so uncomfortable that I would have to excuse myself and escape as soon as I could and go home. It is not a totally rational act, but then not much is when you are experiencing deep grief.

My husband died at home, and the house echoed with emptiness. One would think I wouldn't want to be there, yet I was drawn back there like a magnet. Once home, I was most comfortable being in my bed--I felt safe there. If I could have given in to it, frankly I would have preferred to stay in my bed all day except maybe to go downstairs for meals and venture out to the supermarket. If the market delivered, I could have avoided going out at all. If someone could have cooked and brought my meals to my bedroom on a tray, that would be fine with me, too.

When I awoke in the morning, I forced myself not to stay in the bed all day but made myself get out of bed by 8 a.m., which was just an arbitrary time. I was just lying there anyway having been up since the wee hours of the morning. I only slept on my side of the bed (and I still do). In the morning, I would pull up the quilt and arrange the pillows artfully and in three minutes the bed was made. This way I wasn't so tempted to jump back under the covers again so early in the day. I didn't yearn to get into my bed, necessarily to sleep, I wasn't sleeping very well anyway. The bed became my security blanket where I felt more or less invincible – protected from the pain and chaos I felt out in the world. It was like a cocoon. I had to figure out how to cut my way out of it and start life anew, but I wasn't nearly ready for that, yet. The only time it didn't feel safe was when there was a terrible rain storm, especially if it was accompanied by strong winds, driving rain, thunder, and lightning. Since I was a small child, I was always fearful of storms like this, so it was nothing new. The new part was being there alone listening to the rain pouring on the pitched roof, sounding like a hurricane even if it wasn't and the winds swirling through the trees sounding like a freight train and around the corners of the room as if they were trying to find a space to enter the room. Many people like the sound of the rain pelting on the roof and liken it to a lullaby. I did not want to be there alone, but I had no choice. Once in bed I gathered my eye glasses, newspaper, Kindle, as much pertinent paper work as I could, lists of phone calls to make, my calendar, etc. I piled all those things

70

up on the covers and pillows within easy reach and often the bed became my upstairs office.

My home office was down two flights and I would go there in there in the morning and take care of the paperwork that seemed to pile up daily, most of it related to my husband's death, his now defunct business, and estate. I didn't want to go down there and work on those things. Every morning I suffered from the worst case of inertia, but the sooner that I took care of those things, the sooner I could go upstairs and crawl back into bed. Some days it seemed that there was so much to do, that I never got back into my bed until late afternoon.

For bedtime, I had a different arrangement on the bed. At night I cleared most of my "office supplies" off the bed. I arranged my Kindle, my cell phone, and glasses along with the remote for the TV. I placed them in order, to my right within arm's reach, like a surgeon lines up his instruments. I called this arrangement of items my nighttime kit as opposed to what I kept on the bed during the daytime. This way there was still room in the bed for me. If I couldn't fall asleep or got up in the middle of the night I could have an activity at the ready. I usually wore my reading glasses on a lanyard around my neck. Several times, I had fallen asleep with them on my neck and turned over in the night bending my glass frames beyond repair, so I tried to remember to take them off when I turned the light out. My bedtime (at least the part of getting ready for bed) had become as soon as possible after I finished my dinner and could drag myself up the stairs to my bedroom. The first floor seemed so quiet and devoid of life that I couldn't bear to stay down there in the evening any longer than need be. The house had two master bedrooms; one upstairs, where our bedroom was located, and the other one was on the first floor. Frank died in the first floor bedroom and I still felt his presence. As I passed the door to the bedroom I always felt compelled to peer in to see if he had somehow magically returned.

I don't know if you could call "reading" my hobby, but I am a prolific reader. I rarely go anywhere without a book, and now my e-reader. I am an Aries (if you believe in astrology) so I am a very impatient person and don't like waiting, be it at the doctor's office or at the beauty salon, etc. I think it is a serious waste of time which I can use to read. I often found in the first months after my husband passed away that it was hard to focus on reading for too long, I could barely get through the newspaper, and reading a book was almost impossible. I have always been an inveterate newspaper reader. My husband always read the sports section first and then went for the crossword puzzle before reading the other sections. I am one of those newspaper readers that deconstructs the paper while reading it and leave it a mess, pages not folded back and sections all askew. I can't fold maps either. Perhaps this is a genetic failing. When I finished reading the paper, I always tried to put it back into some form of order so my husband, or the next person, doesn't find it in such a terrible state and can make some sense of the newspaper. Frank rarely complained about the state of the paper after I had read it, but I don't think he quite appreciated my ability to turn the paper into origami. Shortly after he passed away, it occurred to me that I could do whatever I wanted with the newspaper. I could trash the paper all I wanted. Not much of a trade-off.

I also tried reading, light fiction only, no good literature, no books about the Holocaust, violence, depression, alcoholism, drug addiction, suicide or any other kinds of sadness or personal loss, etc. Even then, when I got to the bottom of a book page, I would often think, "What did I just read?" and go back to the top of the page and try again to make some meaningful sense out of what sometimes looked like a jumble of words. Plan A was after re-reading a page two times without comprehending anything, I would close the book and put it aside on the bed to try again later. Plan B was to watch TV, but not just any show, especially in the middle of the night when I couldn't sleep. I became addicted to "Law and Order." Any of the versions of it would do, old or new. I soon learned which cable stations played the re-runs and at what time of day or night. It made no difference to me if I had seen the episode already, although I was surprised how many episodes I had never seen or maybe didn't remember. When "Law and Order," "Law and Order-Criminal Intent," or "Law and Order-Special Victims Unit" were on two different channels at the same time, I had difficulty choosing which one to watch in the franchise, although I began to favor "Law and Order-Criminal Intent." I considered recording one and watching the other, but I thought that might be going too far, so I would switch back and forth between the two shows during commercials. In this way I could actually make some sense of both of them and didn't have to deal with commercials, especially the ones in the middle of the night. I had my own "Law and Order" marathon.

You may wonder about my attraction to "Law and Order" episodic TV. Although I know that many people are great fans of those shows too. I am not really sure why I like those shows so much and used them oftentimes to lull me back to sleep. All three of the shows have a predictable arc of storytelling. Although they usually begin with an act of violence, and occasionally there may be later violence as well, it is not gratuitous violence as the show is really not about violence, but about the criminal justice system. Having worked in the criminal justice system in Philadelphia for many years, I thought it was an interesting version of what really goes on and they always get their "man." I Often would fall asleep after only watching 10 or 15 minutes of the show anyway, but if it caught my interest I would get hooked on the show and watch until it was over, then I was really awake and another "Law and Order" often followed that one so I ended up watching two consecutive hours of the shows, but that was my limit and I had to put on something else like The History or The Discovery Channel, or the overnight or early morning local newscast (which is usually a rehash of the previous evening's news) which soothed me back to sleep. It is like having someone keeping you company who talks in low tones and is boring.

As time went by, I noticed that my relationship with "Law and Order" was losing its grip on me; it was getting monotonous. One night as I perused the channels to find something new to watch that might be mindless and help soothe me into sleep, I came upon a cable channel called HGTV. I think it might come under the umbrella of a "reality" show. It was difficult to read the information on the screen at the end of the show as it was in one of the smallest fonts I have ever seen and it came and went so quickly that it was not possible to read it, nor did I care. It was all about buying, selling, and renovating homes. I am not sure why I found this channel to be helpful to me. It did impart some good information on selling my home and renovating my apartment, even though I was almost past that chapter of my life, I continue to watch it. There is no violence in it and each segment has a certain monotony to it which can be quite soothing. I would watch other cable or regular shows, but this became my fall back show. I can't tell you what I will watch next year. I discovered that many other people I know also are avid HGTV fans and we all seem surprised that we like this mindless show and even find it amusing.

I, for one, have made the decision twice after the traumatic death of my daughter and then my husband 30 years later, to sell my home and move within six months' time. The first time the decision was made in concert with my husband, and the second time the decision was my responsibility alone with input from my husband before he passed away, children and a friend who was also my real estate broker. How do I know that I made the right decision? I don't, except that I still feel comfortable with the route I took. I believe that decisions can only be judged after the fact. Now that I have some space since the sale of my home, I can't see the down side to it or, at least, what difference a year would have made if I had to make the decision today or even two or three years from now. I am not sure I would be any more emotionally able to make a better decision if I had to do it again today. Surely the decision to move, both times, had a large emotional component (as do most real estate transactions involving one's home), but it still would, no matter when I would choose to do it.

We had lived in our home in the tiny hamlet (1,800 year round residents) of Water Mill for ten years. Living on the Eastern Shore of Long Island represented a big change in our lives, having moved away from Philadelphia where we had lived all of our lives where we were born and attended all of our schooling including the University of Pennsylvania. We had gone out to the Hamptons for vacations many times over the last ten years to visit some friends and to see Susan when she was working in the Hamptons as a chef. We loved the beauty of the area as well as the ambience. We bought a small (by Hampton standards) house and rented it out in the summer, planning to retire there in the future. Other than in the summer, we went out for long weekends and enjoyed our time there, even though it was almost a four hour ride from Philadelphia. We used to borrow books on CD's from the local library and listen as we drove. Our home was a lovely cedar shingled cottage that had been built in 1973. We had a flower and a vegetable garden which consisted mostly of tomato plants, and two peach trees, which my husband called his peach orchard. We shared the orchard with the deer and the birds, but they got the bulk of the crop. Frank was intent on growing peaches, especially white peaches. He sprayed and fertilized the trees, put a deer fence around the trees, he even put a special netting over the trees to keep the birds from eating the ripe fruit, but the birds still managed to peck at the juicy peaches through the openings in the netting causing the crop to be inedible. Each year the local wildlife took a bigger toll on the usable (by humans) fruit. Our peach orchard was Frank's science experiment gone terribly wrong. Our property had many other beautiful trees and flowering bushes like my beloved Lilacs, and a view of a very large bucolic horse farm where they played polo on Saturday in the summer. David kiddingly said, "My parents moved to Long Island and became farmers."

Joey and Ella thought it was their "other" home and we all had wonderful times as a family together at the house. Susan and Steve had a house about 15 minutes away and we went over there for July 4th barbecues and celebrated Mother's and Father's Day with home cooked brunches. The time spent with my family is what I miss the most. Six months after I moved away I went back to the Hamptons for my first return visit with my family, I purposely took a detour so I wouldn't see my house. I wasn't ready for that and I don't know if

I will ever be able to drive by it. But the longer I was away from it, the more I looked back through the filter of my memories and it was all good.

I put our house up for sale a month after Frank passed away, as per my husband's wishes. I was pleased to see that the real estate agents did bring a lot of potential buyers. There were 33 showings of the house in just over three months, many days there were multiple showings but nobody bought. The agents always called first, sometimes the day before to make an appointment or sometimes the same day. They preferred that you weren't home when they came by. They didn't want the potential buyer to see the widow lady, me, lying in the bed like Queen Victoria, when they brought people through.

In the morning, I prepared for possible "showings." I would jump quickly out of the bed, straighten up the quilt, throw the pillows on the bed, grab all the things on the bed and shove them under the bed, which had a bed skirt that hid everything. In five minutes, I had the bedroom looking like a show house. When I knew that real estate folks were on their way, I would leave and go to the food market, which was only five minutes away, to buy something for dinner and then sit in the car in the parking lot, reading my Kindle, until the real estate agent called me to say that "the coast was clear" and I could return home. The real estate agent was a friend, and usually he would wait for me and we would have a cup of coffee or tea and a toasted bagel and just talk for a while – I don't think that he ever knew what a kind and thoughtful gesture that was and how much it helped me get through the process of selling my home. There were days when this happened more than once. On some days, I just couldn't get myself together again to go back to the shopping center parking lot. I was there so many times that I thought someone might report me to the police as being suspicious, but they never noticed me. I have mentioned that I often felt invisible and sitting in the car in the parking lot, made me believe that maybe I really was.

On some days, if the weather were nice, I would sit outside my home on a chaise lounge reading the newspaper and not my Kindle. I read the paper so I could peek over it and see the people looking at my house without being too obvious. One day, I had already been to the shopping center parking lot and it was raining so I couldn't sit outside. Instead I sat in the screened eating porch, closer to the action than the real estate agents would have liked. I could not help overhearing this rather unpleasant man making derogatory comments about my home. This is why the real estate agents don't want the seller to be around. Although this man was a potential buyer, based on his remarks and his demeanor, I knew that he didn't want to buy the house.

All he wanted was to get out of there. He remarked in a loud, rather querulous voice, "I thought that you (referring to the real estate agents) told me that this house had a two car garage. That's not a two car garage. Where is the other garage?"

The garage was actually what is sometimes called a one and a half or oversized garage. It could only hold one car, but had room for bicycles, an extra refrigerator, and lots of shelving, but not two cars.

I got up from the porch and stood on the threshold of the dining area and responded to his comment, "It is interesting that you said that. I was wondering about that myself. When I went to bed last night, there was a two car garage, and when I got up this morning the second garage was missing. I have no idea where it went."

Then I excused myself and went back to where I was sitting and continued to read my paper. The two real estate agents rolled their eyes at me and the man did not know what to say. I knew that that the man was not going to buy my house so I thought I might as well have some fun. And, I was right. He didn't have any interest in buying the house even if it had a three car garage.

TIME HAS A NEW DIMENSION

Older women are often accused of driving too slowly due to poor eyesight, a level of dementia, or other physical problems. I think older women, more than older men are often accused of poor driving behaviors. Other drivers honk at them impatiently or sometimes even worse, subjecting them to rude mutterings or the famous finger in the air. If truth be told, I believe that the slow driving can be attributed, in the majority of cases, to the fact that for widows, especially the newly anointed ones, have had their inner clock damaged, at least temporarily.

I noticed time seemed to creep ever so slowly in the first few months after Frank's death and caused me to check my watch constantly as the hands appeared to be stuck. Oh look – its 11:13 a.m., now its 11:14 a.m. and so on throughout the day. No matter what I planned for the day, shopping, doctors' appointments, paperwork (that dreaded paperwork), I adapted to this snails' pace and, therefore I drive much more slowly to match this newly minted rhythm. Really, where am I going? I got in the habit of being early for everything and then having to wait. I carry my Kindle with me so I will have something to do. Once I got used to eating meals again, however simple they may be, they became the highlights of the day. One of my main activities was constantly checking the time, which often seemed to stand still, as I would wend my way to the next meal. Once I finally got to dinnertime, the prize after that was getting into bed, which I had been wanting to do all day, and hopefully to sleep. Once in bed, I found myself checking the time on the bedside clock constantly as the minutes blinked away, midnight, 2:00 a.m., 3:30 a.m., etc. I was sure for the first couple of months that every day contained at least 30 excruciatingly long hours.

It was difficult to get an insight into the chronology of this challenging new life that I did not choose. Every day felt so long. I miss my honey so much and think of him many, many times a day. Yet, when I realized at one point that it was almost ten months since that terrible day, I had wondered where the time had gone. I couldn't believe that time had gone by so quickly. Time was roaring by and standing still at the same time. How can that be? It is all very confusing. At times I felt that I was adrift--never sure if time was racing or crawling. I had very little memory of the first ten months after his death. Where did they all go? I don't remember July, or August, or any of those months by names. I can't anchor any event or activity to a specific day, they all blurred together. Before I got out of bed in the morning I tried to concentrate and to identify which day of the week that it was. They all seemed alike. I had to constantly look in my calendar to actually find out when certain things did occur. The hours, days, nights, weeks, months are all compressed into one measure of time that had no name. Whole blocks of time have evaporated into thin air. It is a new dimension of time, like being thrust into a parallel universe as in science fiction movies.

The issue of time seems to be a common thread among widows. I have never spoken to another widow who didn't bring it up in conversation. For example, "Sometimes I feel like five years have passed and other times it is yesterday," "It seems so very long ago and yet time stands still." Most widows, regardless of how long it has been, offer the following unsolicited comment, part of the widowspeak language, like a line in a script they cannot forget, "It seems like such a long time ago and, yet, just a few minutes ago," and their eyes always tear up. At times I wrote about months, the first month, the tenth month, etc., now I measure this life altering event in terms of years.

THE LISTING OF FIRSTS

As the days, weeks, and months pass, I am cognizant that all of it brings new anniversaries and firsts. It is like the statistics at a baseball game and the announcers keep throwing out at you to keep your interest going. For example, the first anniversary of the pitcher's perfect game or the outfielder's grand slam. Welcome to the new world of grief. Every hour and every day brings a plethora of new firsts or anniversaries. You can always connect something such as, it is three weeks since the first day that Frank started to feel sick, or six weeks since I slept in my house alone for the first time, on and on ad nauseam. I soon realized that others tired of hearing about the anniversaries and firsts. In fact they don't really get the importance of these life markers because some of them seem so trivial. It is usually better to keep it to yourself so I decided to keep a private "first" list. That does not mean that after the first year, the firsts are over, they just turn into seconds, etc.

Whether they relate to time or season, these anniversaries serve as triggers to bring back memories and are often difficult to deal with. Most, but not all anniversaries, are related to the calendar. One of the most difficult firsts is the first year anniversary after the death. Then the next one is the end of the calendar year as the new year approaches. That is the anniversary of the last year, the person was alive. The next December 31st is the anniversary of the first year that the loved one was not there at all. And so it goes.

There is a strange phenomenon related to calendar anniversaries. It seems that the anticipation of the days leading up to the actual date often feels worse than the anniversary date. I call it the "Chicken Little the Sky is Falling" phenomenon. In that children's' tale, there is the painful waiting for the sky to fall which never really falls on the specified day. All that upset for naught. As the first anniversary approached, the pain and anxiety increased and I woke up on that day and nothing earth-shattering occurred. As the day progresses, it is pretty much like any other day. I have learned that it is more of the anticipation of the day, rather than the actual day, that weighed so heavily on my mind.

The loved one's birthday is also a major event. Perhaps even sadder than the other anniversaries is a wedding anniversary. The memories of a marriage are all in the past, and there will be no new ones. What I believe makes it even more difficult is the fact that most family and friends do not remember these dates. As the years go by, fewer and fewer people remember until it is only me, my children, and maybe a smattering of friends that gets smaller with each passing anniversary. But then again, why should they remember? It is unrealistic for me to expect that most people would remember all the special dates, even though I have specifically told some of my closest family and friends that I would appreciate it if on certain anniversary dates that they would call or email me and simply say, "I am thinking of you today."

As time drifted into the second year, I found that I was starting to miss some of these dates to add to my list and only remembered them in hindsight. I would think, "Frank died 18 months ago yesterday and I didn't remember the anniversary." I guess that is a good thing. The list is long enough. Some of the firsts are not very consequential, except to me, like the first time I went to the beach without Frank and got wicked sunburn on my back. In the past, I would apply the sun screen on the areas that I could reach and Frank would say, "Let me put it on your back." I didn't even have to ask and I reciprocated by rubbing the sunscreen on his back. Here I was experiencing another first, a painful one, both from the sunburn and the realization that I could add this to my list of "firsts" like a lot of other insignificant items which are evidence that life has changed.

I married when I was only 19 years old. Until then, I always lived at home, except for five summers at over-night camp. After the children grew up and moved out of the house and Frank often went out of town on an overnight business trip, I would sleep alone in my home, but that is not really being alone. Once in a while, it was nice to have a night by myself, knowing that it is only a night or two and then Frank would return. But the week after the funeral, I was truly alone. Several family and friends mentioned that perhaps it would be difficult for me to stay alone in the house. A number of family and friends made sure to call me at bedtime or in the morning to check on me and to make certain I was surviving. Surprisingly that first night was not an issue. I was comfortable in my bed and in my home by myself. In fact that seemed to be the easiest part of the day, the end of it. I felt safe in my bed. I have lots of beautiful pillows on the bed, and I just removed the ones on my side of the bed and left Frank's side untouched. When Frank and I were wakeful at night, we would turn to the other person to see if they were awake, and we would wave to each other. Sounds silly, but it is just one of the many little, private things that couples develop during a long marriage. Here was a first, that portended to be a problem and wasn't at all.

April 10th, 2011 was my first birthday since Frank's death and the family took me out to dinner to celebrate, a Spungen family tradition. We finished dinner accompanied by the ubiquitous slice of yummy cake with a candle. No need to put the correct number of candles on the cake, the icing might melt. As I went to blow out the candle, everyone said, "Make a wish!" I wondered how I could make a wish when I already knew that my wish couldn't come true. I tried to make a back-up wish, but it was drowned out by the wish I couldn't have. Try as hard as I could, I couldn't formulate an alternate wish so I just pretended.

Two months later was Frank's Yahrtzeit, the first anniversary of his passing on the Jewish calendar. When a person is Jewish, every year you celebrate (not sure if that is the correct word) two anniversaries of a loved one's passing, the actual date and the Jewish calendar date, which has a 13 month cycle. I am not clear if that is a bonus or not. The marking of Jewish holidays, the anniversary of their passing, and other events all begin at sundown the night before. Another part of marking the anniversary is to light a memorial candle at sundown the night before. The candle is in a little glass that has just enough wax to burn for 24 hours, and the wax should then be completely burned out approximately at sundown the next night. The wick and flame are below the top of the glass to protect it from drafts or being a fire hazard.

At sundown I placed the burning candle on a plate in the kitchen. Before I went to bed that night, I checked the candle. The next morning when I went into the kitchen, I was shocked to see the candle was no longer burning, but the glass was still full of wax and the wick was still quite long. It was beyond my understanding how this happened. I have never seen or heard of this before. I relit the candle, which I later found out from a rabbi was not the right thing to do according to the Jewish customs, but this time it burned all the way down. I have no doubt that Frank blew out the candle and was trying to tell me that he was still here and didn't need the candle and I didn't want to believe otherwise. Thinking he was gone was a worse alternative. The next night I went to synagogue to say the Mourner's Kaddish, the prayer for the dead, another first. The rabbi said Frank's name from the pulpit. I had called his office earlier to make that request. The service was comforting, and I found the candle incident strangely calming as I felt his nearness to me. On the second anniversary of his death, Frank did not blow out the candle again.

MOVIES SAVE THE DAY

I have always been a movie buff. When you are suddenly plunged into this new world of being alone, it would seem that going to the movies would be a pleasant time filler. After Frank's death, I discovered that I didn't want to go to the movies by myself. I made an exception about a month after he passed away. The first time I went to the movies alone was to see "Eat, Pray, Love." My daughter Susan had worked as the culinary consultant on the film and had cooked the food that appeared on the screen for the "Eat" portion of the movie. Frank and I were always very proud of her work (sometimes much to her embarrassment) and I thought that would be enough to get me through it. I watched the first section of the movie and my face was wet with tears – tears of joy at her beautiful work and tears because Frank was not there to enjoy seeing it with me and not holding my hand. For almost 54 years, we always held hands in the movies until our hands fell asleep and then we would let go for a short while and then hold hands again.

After the "Eat" section of the movie was over, I would have liked to go home and not see the rest of the movie since Susan's cooking was limited to the first part of the movie, but then I would have missed her screen credits, so I stayed to the end. Her credits took forever to come onto the screen and by then, I was the only person left in the movie theatre except for two teenagers sweeping up the usual detritus off the floor. They were sneaking sideward glances at me and cleaning in a wide circle around me. They were probably thinking, "Who is this crazy lady who refuses to leave and why is she crying?" Finally, Susan's credit came up on the screen for a nanosecond. I was catapulted out of my seat and I said in a moderate voice, "Yeah! Susan," and put two thumbs up. As I turned around to leave the theatre, the tears started to trickle down my face again. I heard an audible sigh of relief from the floor sweepers as they watched me exit the theater.

A few weeks later, I made another attempt to go to the movies by myself on a lovely sunny summer afternoon. I did not feel like going to the beach or to the movies, but I felt the need to go out and not sit home alone, so the movies it was. Unfortunately, Sag Harbor, this lovely little town in the Hamptons does not offer many public parking spaces for more than two hours which greatly limits the movies that you can see in that short time span (including walking to and from the parking areas). They are very strict about this and mark your car tires with colored chalk with a secret code to indicate what time your two hours are up. This activity is carried out and monitored by teenagers called Traffic Control Officers who are dressed in brown outfits that strongly resemble the uniforms worn by Italian soldiers during World War II. The officers constantly patrol every inch of space looking for violators (maybe they earn a commission). To make matters worse, parking tickets in Sag Harbor are quite expensive and must be paid in cash or with a money order, no checks or credit cards are accepted. After checking the movie run time, I found one of the few three hour spots in a small parking lot that would allow me the short walk to the theater, to watch the movie, and get back to my car in time and not get a ticket. I kept one eye on the movie and the other on my watch to make sure that I had enough time. Not a good way to focus on a movie. As soon as it was over, I did not wait for the credits (Susan didn't do the cooking for this movie) and walked quickly to the car.

I got there with eight minutes to spare. Instead of a sigh of relief, I was shocked to see a parking ticket on the car, a very expensive ticket for two different illegal parking violations. One was for parking for more than two hours in a three hour spot. How could that be? Maybe the parking team couldn't count to three. The other was for parking on a crosswalk. On inspection, I observed that the entire parking lot had no crosswalks. I saw a uniformed police officer sitting in his SUV. I hadn't cried during this movie; I actually thought it was terrible, but now I was crying out of anger and frustration. I showed him the ticket and he agreed that I had done nothing wrong, but he said, "I am not a Traffic Control Officer, and if I were, I would tear up the ticket. Go to the Police station on Monday morning at 9:00 a.m., ask for the Police Chief, and he should be able to take care of it."

I took some pictures of the alleged violations on my phone and went home. On Monday morning, after a sleepless night, I went back to

Sag Harbor and found the new police station which was hidden away down an alley (a picturesque one, but an alley nonetheless). A clerk wearing an official police uniform, about two sizes too big that looked more like a Halloween costume on her, was sitting behind a large pane of bullet proof glass. I know police have to be safe, but other than a few drunken and disorderly citizens, there is little or no violent crime in this picturesque little town. I thought maybe such a wide swath of bullet proof glass was a little over the top.

After explaining my dilemma and asking to speak with the Police Chief, the clerk gave me a sharp rebuff, "The Chief is not here and everyone says they didn't park illegally and I believe my employees more than I believe you. I will take this down to one of the officers on duty. Wait here." She wouldn't even look at my pictures.

About ten minutes later she returned waving the ticket in the air.

"I am going to let you go this time."

I was going to ask for a receipt or something official in case they sent me summons in the mail, but I thought better of it, and muttered, "Thank you."

I backed out of the door and ran as fast as I could before the lady in the police costume could change her mind. That pretty much ended my going to the movies alone for the next year. I decided it was safer to watch movies at home on TV.

I know that many people go to the movies alone, usually by choice or for a variety of other reasons. Some people tell me that they don't like to go to the movies alone and not for any special reason. One day I was discussing my movie issues with some friends who were very accepting of my decision not to go to the movies alone for a while. "They" did not give me suggestions on how I should handle this issue. Another woman in the group in her late 60's, who had never been married, but was very social and outgoing said, "When I want to go to the movies, if I don't have a date or no one else is available to join me, I go alone. I have done it for years. It is not a big deal."

Her judgmental attitude wounded me and I realized that she didn't get it at all. I dropped the topic and did not discuss anything personal in her presence again. I guess I should be more patient with people who have not walked in my shoes.

One Sunday afternoon almost 18 months after Frank's passing, I wanted to see the movie "Hugo" on a Sunday afternoon. There was no one around to go with so off I went, at the last minute, BY MYSELF. I enjoyed it and I never gave it too much thought except to realize that I had moved on when it came to going to the movies alone. Not sure if this was going to be a standing precedent, but I would just wait and see what I would do the next time I wanted to go to the movies and there was no one to accompany me. A few months later, I wanted to see the movie, "The Descendants." I am a dyed in the wool George Clooney fan. I have liked some of his movies better than others, but I have never seen one that I didn't like. I was beginning to realize that if I went to the movies alone, I was free to stay or leave, or even cry. Maybe that wasn't so bad.

A woman, of a certain age came in just as the show started. I was sitting on the aisle seat and she excused herself as she went past me, leaving one seat open between us. I smiled at her and she turned to face me and said, "I am a widow and I always went to this movie theater with my husband and this is the first time I am going to the movies alone."

I nodded and asked, "How long ago did your husband die?"

"Five years ago," she responded.

"My husband died a year ago." I am not even sure why I said that – maybe to make her feel more comfortable.

I discovered that nobody pays any attention to whatever you are doing, as long as you don't speak, kick the back of the seat in front of you, send text messages, or make a lot of noise as you rustle the candy wrappers. I really enjoyed the movie and as it ended and the lights came on again, my movie partner and I introduced ourselves. Her name was Lenore and she said, "I made it through the movie and enjoyed it very much and I think having you sit near me, gave me the strength to do it."

I told her, "I feel the same."

I noticed a neighbor sitting in front of me. She, too, had been widowed and was sitting alone. She came over to join us in conversation.

I am sorry that I didn't ask Lenore for her phone number, maybe we could have gone to the movies together. I have looked for her in the movies ever since. I hope she was able to go to the movies again, either alone or found someone to join her. We could have started a movie club for bereft widows who find it difficult, or even impossible, to go to the movies alone.

A few months later I went to see "The Help" It was playing at the same nearby neighborhood movie. I couldn't wait to see it. Someone else asked me to join them, but I wanted to see it solo. This time I made specific plans to go by myself as it just seemed an enjoyable activity to do on a quiet Sunday afternoon. I took myself to the movie and laughed out loud. I loved the movie, and there was no sadness about going by myself. Bottom line, it would have been better if Frank had gone with me, but I accepted that was not to be. I realized that I was making major progress. I was, again, hoping that this step would be permanent and I can check this off my list of fears to face.

THE BRIDGE IS BROKEN

After Frank died I started to have panic attacks. I have renamed them, "missing my honey" attacks. I became fearful of doing most anything alone. These anxieties were new behavior for me, or at least, the depths of them were new. My heart boomed in my chest. I felt as if I couldn't breathe, loud noises like the telephone ringing startled me. I had flashbacks, nightmares, and could not sleep more than two hours at a time. It sounds very similar to Post Traumatic Stress Disorder (PTSD) and maybe it is part of that syndrome. I think all the loss, pain, and trauma experienced in one's life (and who hasn't been touched by some of it?) accumulates over time. A new event might be just enough to push us to the tipping point and hit the wall. Some of us are more resilient than others and some of us need more time and/or support to process life's changes as new events occur and append themselves to earlier ones. This process is sometimes called bouncing back. It all gets rolled into one big ball and it is hard to discern where it all begins or if there is an end to it. And some of us need some professional help in working this all through. Good friends and family can help, but they do not always understand, partly because we do not open up our deepest thoughts and feelings to them in fear that they may find it too emotionally overwhelming and will turn away from us. Many close family and friends want to help, but offer unsolicited advice, which may not be useful. If I am going to confide in someone, I tell them what I want beforehand - that I just want them to listen and nod their head, or I want them to offer some response—an opinion, to brainstorm with me, but not to interrupt me. This way we start off with a level playing field.

It seems that most of my panic attacks occurred before activities that I had always done with Frank, like driving places (he almost always drove while I served as the chief navigator and DJ), going shopping or other errands, or doctors' appointments. I never realized all the things I didn't do by myself. I was surprisingly less independent, in certain ways, than I thought I was. When I worked, I traveled all over the country and did a lot of public speaking all by myself and was quite successful in my career. Now I was both driver and navigator, in all aspects of my life, and I didn't feel qualified or safe doing either. In the early weeks after Frank's death, I noticed that I occasionally still approached the car from the passenger side as if I were expecting Frank to get in on the driver's side, but I would realize my error and casually walk around to the driver's side in case somebody was watching me. I soon gave that up along with the DJ job.

In the interim, I had developed a great fear of getting lost if I went more than a few miles from my home and especially if I was unfamiliar with the area. I would use the GPS in my car, I would print out MapQuest for my destination, and I would get written directions from several people. I successfully managed to get to my destination, but often didn't even get out of the car. Instead, I turned around and went back home again because I was so anxious that I might not remember how to get back, even in broad daylight. One day, I headed to the mall to go to Bloomingdales in King of Prussia, a suburb near Philadelphia. I had the GPS and a pile of written instructions on the seat next to me, but my memory kicked in. Even though I hadn't been there for more than 10 years, I easily found my way, an even better route than the GPS and others had recommended. I had gone to Bloomingdales to look for quilts for the beds in my new guest room and once I completed my errand, I hurried out to the parking lot and headed home. I did not linger in the other departments or go to any other stores as I was afraid to push my luck and not be able to find my way home.

Two years after Frank's death (yes, it took me that long) I made plans to drive to the South Jersey shore to visit some friends for a few days and to do that, I had to drive over the Benjamin Franklin Bridge which connects Philadelphia and Camden, New Jersey. I have driven over that bridge many, many times, but I rarely drove over the bridge solo as I usually had my driver--Frank. I pictured the bridge would abruptly end in the middle and I would go flying off into space like in the movie, "Thelma and Louise," but I couldn't find someone to play Thelma to my Louise. I tried to do new things by myself and there were numerous things that I discovered were easy, but I found many things difficult and I didn't like it. It was the journey that was uncomfortable and not the end point. I ran the risk of having a panic attack or avoiding doing certain things and just isolate myself and become agoraphobic – it is often tempting to just stay home where I felt safe. I read a newspaper article recently about driving over bridges that amazed me as there seems to be a lot of people who find driving over bridges by themselves a frightening and often impossible task. At some places in this country, there are professional drivers that can be hired on either side of certain very high bridges to drive people who have this very same problem. A person can even make a reservation for a driver! The rules usually state that the passenger can sit up front with the driver or in the back seat, but not ride in the trunk. The article noted that often people who fear driving across bridges have experienced traumas in their lives. I found that fact a revelation as I thought that I was the only one who had the bridge issue and felt better knowing that it was not an uncommon problem. Discovering that I was sharing this quirky behavior with other people, not just widows, made me feel a lot better, like it was an almost ordinary behavior and that I wasn't crazy.

One day I received an unsolicited booklet in the mail from AARP dealing with the topic of widowhood (How did they know that Frank died? Maybe they got the information from Social Security like the credit card companies). It contained quite a bit of helpful and important material. One of the subjects listed was the development of panic attacks in the aftermath of the death of a loved one, especially a spouse or partner. The article recommended that this might require the help of a professional and not just the passage of time or attending a support group to address the panic attacks. I thought that this was a good recommendation and I made a note to follow up on this suggestion.

I continued to read through the booklet glancing at other topics. There was a discussion of safe driving and its importance especially when a person is feeling disoriented, has panic attacks when driving, is a senior citizen, or was not the primary driver in the family before being widowed. Did they mean me? It was suggested that the reader consider taking the AARP "Safe Driving" course that would be helpful in brushing up driving skills and consequently make a person feel more confident behind the wheel as well as a better and safer driver. I was familiar with the AARP course as Frank and I had taken the eight-hour, two-day course twice over the last six years primarily to receive the perk of a 5% discount on our auto insurance for three years. I checked my files and realized that it was more than three years since I had last taken the course and my safe driver discount would be running out this year. As long as I had retained a copy of the last safe driving certificate as proof it had been completed less than four years ago, I qualified for the new four hour version of the class designed for people who had taken the class before. I wasn't particularly busy at this juncture of my life and it seemed a worthwhile way to spend a half day, feeling that if my driving skills were updated it might make me more comfortable behind the wheel. I also thought the 5% discount for my car insurance for the next three years would come in handy. I immediately got on-line and signed up for the next class held in my area-- and the best part--it still only cost $10.00.

The next Thursday, a beautiful sunny day in early November, I packed a snack, a bottle of water, and a few pencils and drove to the class which was being held in a nearby senior citizen activities center. The class was in a large multi-use room with six round tables. When I arrived I found the course materials were arranged neatly on the tables: each set with a red folder, an AARP Safe Driving Handbook, an AARP book mark, and a red AARP pencil to match. I was early and chose a seat. By 1:30 p.m., six other people had shown up which surprised me as it had been my experience in the past that these classes were usually fully booked with a maximum of fifteen students. Two couples were seated at one of the tables; my two companions at my table were a man in his 90's who was most concerned about being late for a dinner date he had at 5:45 p.m. with a female friend, and a woman in her fifties, whom I shall call "Dottie" and who was very argumentative about things she clearly knew nothing about. The class was scheduled to run from 1:30 p.m. to 5:30 p.m. At exactly 1:30 p.m. the instructor, an elderly gentleman (who I later found out was in his mid-eighties), made a grand entrance. The instructor, whom I will refer to as, "Bill," an AARP trained volunteer introduced himself to the class in his best professorial voice. He had some kind of odd accent, not foreign or a speech impediment, and I could only understand every fourth word. I still don't know what "analog brakes" are. Bill was a tad cranky and treated us all like little children. He made sure we all knew that he had the power in the class room. He immediately engaged in a hollering contest with Dottie who hollered back at him. This continued throughout the class as the two of them agreed on nothing. This interaction helped alleviate some of the extreme boredom of the next four hours and kept, at least me, awake and sometimes entertained. The first argument began when Dottie had brought a check for $10.00 to pay her fee, and Bill told her that the payment had to be in cash. She didn't agree.

"I have taken this class many times before and I didn't have to pay cash."

Warfare between the two of them escalated throughout the four hours. The issue of the $10.00 was resolved by another participant kindly offering to take a check from the woman in exchange for giving her $10.00 in cash to pay her registration fee. And now that all the bookkeeping was complete we could begin the class.

Bill informed us that the four-hour course used the same handbook and curriculum as the eight-hour class did, but we just went faster and skipped material. The way Bill explained it all made sense to me.

"I will read everything from the book out loud because I can't take the time for you all to read the information, because you probably read too slowly," he said.

As you might imagine, the program was given at warp speed. There were a series of short videos featuring safe driving scenarios that were so scary and depressing that I was considering never driving again, let alone finishing the class. Each video was followed by a series of true-false questions to fill out in the workbook. Bill thought it was taking us too long to put a check mark in the right place in the workbook so we called out the answers. We were picking up speed. My classmates, except for Dottie, had all been driving more than sixty years. Strangely enough, other than Dottie and me, none of them ever spoke or moved from their chairs or went to the rest room. I, on the other hand went to the rest room twice. I don't know what they knew that I didn't--maybe they refrained from drinking all liquids for the hours preceding the class. Bill digressed from the curriculum several times to show us some helpful hints about life, in general, such as his exercise routine that he did for a half an hour every morning before arising from his bed.

By the end of the third hour I was so bored that I began to act in a childish and rude manner, keeping my cell phone in my lap (against Bill's rules) and sending and receiving emails and texts. I did not get caught. When I sent my son an email, he did admonish me and said,

104

"I am going to tell on you."

The course was supposed to finish at 5:30 p.m. when the certificates to be completed for the insurance company were distributed. This keeps everyone from leaving early. The previous times that I had taken the course, this process was begun a little earlier so we could actually leave by 5:30 p.m. Not in Bill's class--he did not begin to wind up the class until the dot of 5:30 p.m. and then and only then, did he distribute the forms and a pen to each of us. He instructed us to fill the forms out line by line and we could not go ahead of his directions. The form had three sheets and carbon paper. Who remembers carbon paper? Bill would walk around and make sure that we pressed very hard with our pens so the writing went through the carbon paper and would show clearly on the last page. We could not go to the next page until Bill had carefully checked each person's page. The man next to me was about to explode because he was afraid he would not make his dinner date on time. Finally, it was over and we were released. It was a rather long four hours, but I am glad that I attended because I did pick up some safe driving pointers which helped to reduce some of my anxiety behind the wheel although I still wasn't up to driving across any bridges. I was entertained by much of the activities of the afternoon and had quite a few private laughs. I definitely got my $10.00 worth. Now when I drive and feel anxious, I remember Bill and his Safe Driving class and it helps lessen the angst.

DREAM THEMES

I have had a number of dreams about Frank after he passed away. They all have the same theme: searching and yearning, which represents one of the early stages of grief. I cannot say that the dreams were in the category of nightmares, but very upsetting nonetheless. They were very real, and stayed with me all day whether my eyes were open or not. It was as if it was a movie that kept running on a loop all day long.

In the first dream, I was wandering around somewhere and looking for Frank in a crowd of people on a lawn. I suddenly heard my son, David, call out to me, "Mom, Dad isn't dead, he was just away on a vacation." I looked up and saw him coming towards me from the outer perimeter of the group. I got a glimpse of him as our eyes met, and he looked fine, and then I was awake. I tried to go back to sleep and continue the dream and have the opportunity to hug him and welcome him home, but it was not to be.

The second dream had to do with a greeting that we used when one or the other came home from shopping, the gym, or other errands and walked in the front door. We knew the other person was home, but not in sight. In the dream, I was upstairs in the bathroom and I heard Frank yell, "Lucy, I'm home" in his best Ricky Ricardo accented voice. Frank had a great ear for accents. If I was the one returning home, I would walk in and call to him, "Ricky, I'm home" in my Lucy voice. It was just a little game we played. That dream was so real that I jumped out of bed and rushed to the top of the stairs, "I am up here, honey" and peered down to see him. He wasn't there, but his Ricky voice continued to echo around the house the rest of the day.

The third dream was similar. I found myself, once more, in a very large group of people in a very fancy ballroom. I had come with Frank, but we had become separated in the crowd and I was walking around looking for him. There was a lot of noise in the room, people talking and laughing loudly. A woman whom I did not know was standing very close to me.

I asked her, "Do you know where Frank went?" She bent close to me and answered in a low whisper, which was drowned out by the noise in the room. I asked her several more times and still could not hear her response. I was getting very frustrated.

Finally, I thought she said, "He went to the bathroom," but I wasn't sure.

"Did you say Frank went to the bathroom?" I woke up before she replied so I was searching all day for Frank and I never did find him.

I had another repetitive dream for a number of years prior to Frank's illness, and continued to have it occasionally over the years. Frank had been a heavy smoker, three packs a day, for more than thirty years. He stopped once for two years and went back to smoking for a few years and then he stopped for five years and resumed smoking and then stopped again about thirty years before his death. The last time, he had resumed smoking, I was very angry with him for doing so. I guess it was easy for me to be angry at his resumption of smoking as I never smoked. I would have the exact same dream intermittently that he had started to smoke again even though he hadn't and I always woke angry. Eighteen months after he passed away, I had the dream and I woke up furious with him for smoking again. I don't know if his smoking was connected to the Pancreatic Cancer. I felt guilty all day for being angry with him since he was deceased, but that dream has not come back so I guess I made peace with that issue.

Frank has continued to populate my dreams, but he more or less floats through them as if he belongs there. The dreams are not as vivid as they were in the time frame closer to his death and usually do not haunt me all day. At times, I even welcome his presence, kind of like a visit.

Step Two in the AARP Handbook was how to address high levels of anxiety which contribute to panic attacks. Contacting a therapist was the primary recommendation. I made contact with an agency, "Fighting Chance" in the Hamptons that specialized in working with cancer patients and their families. I was referred to them by my primary care physician. Although I had not had any prior contact with the agency while my husband was sick, the counselor that took my call, Karrie, made an appointment to see me the next day. I was truly shell shocked and willing to do anything that might alleviate my pain (or bring my husband back). I had worked for many years in a criminal court setting in Philadelphia and ran a support group for people who had a family member murdered, often referred to as "co-victims" of homicide. I felt like I had a real understanding on the experience of grief and bereavement as a result of my daughter's murder, as well as having gone back to graduate school at Bryn Mawr Graduate school of Social Work and getting a Masters of Social Service and a Masters of Law and Social Policy. I had written the definitive college text book on the subject of homicide and traumatic grief and conducted trainings on the subject for professionals. I was able to come up with innovative treatment protocols and interventions that were helpful to this population.

It quickly became clear to me that even though I brought all this knowledge to the table, I couldn't help myself and I wasn't even sure if anyone else could help me. I also realized that many of the things that I told my clients about traumatic grief, when viewed from my new perspective, were less than helpful. I didn't tell them anything wrong, but it wasn't always right either. For example, I would often recommend a client to go to counseling, a level beyond which I could offer as a victim advocate.

The response to such a suggestion was often, "What can they do in counseling to help me? It is over, he is dead and they can't bring him back."

My answer usually was, "But they can walk with you in your pain." That is true and it can be helpful, but it does not always feel like enough. What you really want is for them to fix what is broken. When I went to see the therapist, I asked, begged, cajoled her to bring my husband back, but it was not possible. Her services were free, but I would have paid her if that would make a difference. I wanted Karrie to fix it. Nothing less than that was acceptable. I felt angry and frustrated that the therapist was not capable of acceding to my demands.

I saw the therapist several times. I mostly sat and cried. I don't really remember anything we talked about. I felt safe with Karrie and kept hoping against hope that she would be able to grant my wish and bring my husband back to me. She only worked part-time and could not see me on a regular weekly basis so she suggested that I try going to a support group for new widows that was being formed under the auspices of a local church. There was a torrential thunder storm the night of the first session. I couldn't see where I was going, and I was trying, and not being too successful at it, not to have a panic attack. I left early to give me time to get lost, and I arrived there an hour before anyone else. Finally two gentlemen arrived; they were the support group leaders, and then one other widow came. The two men, Steve and Ed, were rectors at their Catholic church and had gone through a training program to be support group leaders for people whose spouses had died, but were not professional counselors and held other full-time jobs. I don't know if they had ever led such a group before. They said that several other people had committed to coming, but I guess the rain and their anxiety kept them away. I wasn't sure how well this would work. At the end of the session, they gave us some handout material to take home and read before the next session. I looked down at the papers in my hand and realized that I had compiled the same information for the handbook I had written when I was leading professional trainings some years before, but I accepted the printed pages and didn't say anything. I felt that this group was not for me, but I thought that I would give it another try as I wanted, so badly, for someone or something to help me.

The second session was in a different venue, in the church rectory and closer to my home. It was storming again, but I easily found it without having a full-blown panic attack. The entrance to the rectory was up a few steps to a small porch covered with an overhang. An AA meeting was going on at the same time in the building and a group of about ten people all clustered on the small roofed porch, smoking cigarettes, chatting amicably, and trying to stay out of the rain. At each step, choking from the cigarette smoke and trying to get in out of the rain, I pushed through the group,

"Excuse me! Excuse me!" until I finally got into the building through the haze of smoke.

When I went into the room where the support group was to be held, only one other person was there, Ed, one of the leaders from the first week.

"Steve will not be here tonight as he was in an automobile accident and isn't well enough to come, and I haven't heard from the other woman. Why don't we wait for a few more minutes before we start, maybe she will still show up."

We sat and chatted about innocuous topics such as where we grew up and went to school, and how we ended up living in the Hamptons. Finally, we agreed that the other woman was probably not coming and we should begin. Now I was in a support group with one leader (Ed) and one attendee (me); two people does not a support group make. I think that is called therapy.

Ed was a very earnest and sincere person who was trying to do his best to make my life a little better. Things took a surprising 180 degree turn within the first 10 minutes when Ed began to talk about his family, which made me wonder where he was going with this conversation. He brought up some personal family issues that were obviously painful to him. He proceeded to tell me that his father was an alcoholic and sometime in the last few years his grown sister had committed suicide and he had found her body. I kept thinking, "This is not about you," but I couldn't say that to him, so I sat and listened, nodding my head as he talked. Now who was the supporter and who was the supported? When we got to the end of our allotted time, I had not spoken very much because I didn't want to interrupt Ed. He gave me more handouts and I told him that I would not be there for the next session as I was going into Brooklyn to visit my family. As it got closer to the following week's group, I grappled with my quandary. I didn't want to attend the next session as I didn't think it would do either of us any good.

Finally I telephoned him, "Ed, I don't think this group is right for me, but I don't want to let you down." I hope you can start another group and more people will come."

Then I dithered on nervously for a few more minutes and said goodbye. I never saw Ed again, but he worked in the same office with a friend of mine and he used to ask for me and sent his regards via my friend.

I continued to search for support. My son David made a commitment to honor his father by going daily (except on the Sabbath) to a Minyon, a group of a minimum of 10 Jewish men who meet to say Kaddish (the Jewish prayer for the dead). He went wherever he was, home in Brooklyn, traveling on a business trip, visiting in the Hamptons, or in his office building in Manhattan. David was always able to find where a nearby Minyon was being held by Googling it. Modern technology and ancient religious customs meet.

After attending a Minyon in the Hamptons several times, the Rabbi who led the Minyon spoke to David,

"Who are you reciting Kaddish for?"

"My father died on July 2nd."

Rabbi Aron asked David some other questions, "Do you have a mother?"

"Yes."

"How is she doing?"

"Not too well."

"Do you think she would mind if I called her and make an appointment to go and see her?

"I'll ask her and let you know."

When David got home he explained about the Rabbi's offer to come to see me. I had no objections as I thought I should further investigate the spiritual dimension of this terrible event. I think that I would have been willing to talk to any spiritual person, regardless of their religion if they could offer me some help. David called the rabbi, who, in turn called me and we made an appointment for the next week. He arrived promptly and we seated ourselves at right angles on the sofa and the love seat in the den. He was a portly man with a beard, who had a sweet and kind face. He explained some of the religious and spiritual components and ramifications of my husband's death, and I was finding it a very calming and peaceful conversation.

"Have you any future plans?" he asked.

"I plan to sell my house, sooner than later, and I am almost sure I will move back to Philadelphia."

"Do you have any other children besides your son?"

"I have a daughter, Susan, and I had another child, Nancy, who died."

He proceeded to ask me more questions about Nancy and the circumstances of her death. Then he said, "I had a little girl that was very sick, for a long time with meningitis, and then she died," he said.

His pleasant face was now creased with grief. He told me all about his little daughter and the circumstances of her illness and death. Again the tables were turned and the supporter became the supported. Rabbi Aron talked about his daughter for a while and I listened and was witness to his pain and grief. Then he concluded our visit as we stood by the door, to bid our goodbyes.

"I wish I could give you a hug, but, as you know, my religion (an orthodox sect of Judaism) forbids me to touch a woman who is not my wife, but inside, I am sending you a big hug," he said and smiled and left.

I was very moved by his words. He called me weekly for several months to see how I was doing. He always started our conversation by asking, "Did you sell your house, yet?"

I thought it was rather touching that he asked me about the realities of life before he talked about the spiritual issues. I never saw Rabbi

Aron again. He comforted me at our one meeting and maybe, my listening to his story was in some way also helpful to me too. Just like when I was listening to Ed tell me of his pain, I felt somehow empowered knowing that I was able to offer some support as well. I guess I have been the supporter for so many years to others, that I send off signals that gives permission for people to tell me about their own sadness as my public persona doesn't appear to be as fragile as I feel and I have learned to be a very good listener.

The staff from the hospice that took care of Frank had been calling me with regularity to check in to see how I was faring on my journey. One of the phone volunteers told me about a new widows' support group that was forming in the next two weeks and asked me if I were interested in attending.

I asked prior to making a decision whether or not to attend, "How many widows do you think will be there?" The reply, "Eight to ten and they are all newly bereaved in the last year."

"How many leaders?"

"Two, a hospice nurse, Lynn, and a social worker, Gail."

I was still searching for some type of program that might be helpful to me, although I was beginning to have my doubts that I would find some venue that would suit my needs. What I really wanted was someone or something that would bring my husband back, and I was beginning to realize that might not be possible, but I could still try. I am, if nothing else relentless, and off I went hoping that this group would work for me and I would find some personal benefit beyond helping others. Two weeks later I showed up at the first meeting, feeling somewhat optimistic. The support group met at two in the afternoon in a conference room. Nine women were there, including me, and the two group leaders. As each one entered the room, we nervously eyed one another and tentatively smiled. Lynn and Gail explained the rules, which tended to be mostly about privacy issues. We began by going around the room and introducing ourselves and then briefly talking about our husbands and the circumstances surrounding their deaths. Some talked more than others and many cried. This group was structured with enough people to take advantage of the group process. As the meeting continued, I realized that Lynn and Gail took a very low-key approach and almost made it a self-directed group. I felt that at times the group lagged and some people seemed to have lost interest if they were not telling their own stories. Listening can be very upsetting as each story can be worse than the other and difficult to witness. Not that this is the wrong method to run a group, it is only one of the myriad of possibilities. Based on my own experience, as a group leader and trainer for others on how to run groups that focus on grief and bereavement, I felt that there should be more encouragement to get the members to interact with each other and move away from just telling the stories.

I started to realize that I had slipped into more of a leadership role in the meeting, much as I had done at the other meetings. Having many years of experience leading support groups for people who have had a family member murdered, I had adapted a somewhat different technique for leading a group. The pace of the meeting picked up and the women seemed more relaxed and were speaking up. This is not to say that their support group structure is not a good one, just different from my style. I encourage more interaction, but members are free to sit quietly as suits their own needs. It isn't the right or wrong way to conduct a meeting, just a different way. Lynn and Gail didn't seem perturbed by my actions, or at least, they didn't intervene or stop me. By the time the meeting was over, I understood that I had succeeded in wresting control of the meeting away from their model and felt I owed them an apology. I waited until everyone left except Lynn and Gail. I approached them,

"I am really sorry that I kind of took over the meeting and intruded into your domain."

They knew that I had a strong background in the field and seemed very accepting of my actions and thought the meeting went very well and they didn't seem to mind. I didn't go back again as I was not comfortable, and I think that Lynn and Gail were probably relieved that they had their support group back to run as they wished. This was nothing like my previous experiences, but I still hadn't found a comfortable place for me. I fall into the same category as doctors who are often accused of being bad patients, it is just too difficult to let go of your own professional persona. But it is a learning situation to be on the other side and to better understand the experience from a different perspective. In some ways maybe I knew too much to help myself.

THE FINE ART OF "PINGING"

I called Karrie at Fighting Chance and told her what happened every time I tried to connect with a counselor or a group. She wasn't surprised nor were most of my friends. I began to believe that I wasn't going to get anywhere with that. This was part of my journey and I could only persevere in my continued search for the right place for me.

Karrie said, "Deb, be patient." Patience is not one of my strengths, I am an Aries after all. "I am working on putting a support group together that I think will be just what you need. It is a small group of women whose husbands have died from cancer in the last six months and one woman's husband died a year ago. I think you all are going to be a special match. As soon as I have it put together, I will give you a call."

"When do you think it will start?"

"I am working on it, but I promise it will be within the month."

I was out of options so I guess I couldn't do anything but wait. I had been searching for something and I didn't know it if it even existed. My homicide co-victims (family and friends of a homicide victim) were right, "Why should I go to counseling if they can't fix it." But I had to be optimistic, so I felt I should press on.

121

Karrie kept her word. She called me back three weeks later and invited me to the newly organized support group which was to be held in the Fighting Chance offices. It was only about a fifteen minute drive from my home. The meeting was to be held from 1:30 p.m. to 3:00 p.m. so I didn't have to worry about having a panic attack while driving at night, usually in a torrential downpour. I got to the Fighting Chance Office twenty minutes early--I was afraid that somehow I would be delayed in traffic (on a two-lane country road) and I might be late for the meeting. I was so anxious about arriving late that I couldn't find the door into the building. Finally, I made it up to their office and sat by myself munching on pretzels that had been put out on the table. I was so early that no one else had arrived. Obviously others were not as anxious as I was or didn't exhibit it in the same way. The room had been decorated to emulate someone's living room in a lovely beach house. There was even a water view. The walls had white painted wainscoting; the windows were hung with colorful printed café curtains; and there were comfortable sofas slip covered in white cotton muslin with bright pillows and heavy knitted blankets thrown over the backs of the sofas. Karrie came in with the other social worker, Connie. Then in quick succession the other women walked in and greeted the social workers and sat down. I realized that they all knew Karrie and Connie because the women and their husbands had received services from the agency when their husbands were ill, but they did not all know each other. We all greeted each other without too much emotion.

After the introductions by Karrie and Connie, I don't remember who spoke first. I started to cry almost immediately, and I was later told by the others that my tears gave them permission to show emotion as well. I surprised myself with the tears as I hadn't cried much since Frank died. I had finally found a place that felt safe, whether I showed tears or laughter. It was OK in this room. Although the session was only supposed to last 90 minutes, no one seemed ready to leave. Karrie and Connie had to go to other appointments, but let us use the room as long as we wanted. Finally, one by one we all left. As I drove home, I knew that Karrie was right, she had chosen carefully. We were more than just a sisterhood or a committee (as one of the other women had called us) of widows, there had been something special about the chemistry in the room. A strong bond had been immediately formed. I was humbled to be in the company of these beautiful, strong women. They were truly awesome. We would be there the next week which was going to be the last of our weekly sessions, but we would meet again in a month. We asked Karrie and Connie if we could keep meeting weekly. They were not available to be there because of other work commitments, but we were welcome to continue to use the room if we wanted. At the second session, I started crying right away and was not uncomfortable in doing so; it seemed the natural and spontaneous thing to do. I thought, "I felt I had permission from everyone in the room to show my emotions and to say whatever I was feeling and they felt the same."

We all borrowed strength from each other, like cups of sugar, and returned it whenever the other person needed it. One day at a meeting, it was very cold outside and I was wearing one of Frank's sweaters. It was royal blue cashmere, very soft and comforting. Yes, it was quite large on me, but I wore it like a tunic and belted it--how chic. One of the other women walked in with the exact same sweater. We looked at each other and smiled as we both were wearing our husbands' sweaters and knew we felt comforted and embraced by its warmth. The next meeting was in December and sadly that was my last official session as I would be moving back to Philadelphia by the end of the month. I was very sorry to be leaving my sisterhood behind; I would miss them, and do continue to miss them so much. We all bonded in a very special way.

In addition to the regularly scheduled meetings over the next few months, the sisterhood had begun to meet on a monthly basis in each other's homes for pot luck dinners and to continue the connection. I returned for visits during the next two summers and joined them for evenings of friendship and support. Another one of the group moved away the following year, so then there were four, and then there were three, but the group goes on thanks to the Internet and the monthly dinners. For the first year or two rarely did a week go by when we were not all emailing each other, and if there is a silence for more than a week or two one of us jumps on line to check in. Almost all our emails go to the entire group. Our emails celebrate good happenings in our lives and with our families as well as sharing sadness and difficult times. The anniversaries of our husband's deaths come fairly close to each other on the calendar, and we share our happy memories on email or ask for the support of the group if that is what we need. So often, we are all on the same page at the same time. Within minutes of an email going out to the group, responses start to roll back in. I think that most of us have iPhones so we all hear the "pings" of the responses coming in one after the other and, often the thread goes on for the whole day and into the next until we have exhausted ourselves. We all know that something is up, good or bad, or just a need to reach out for contact, when the "pinging" starts. I define pinging as the new technological shorthand for saying, "We are here for you." It is a call for a spontaneous on-line support group meeting. Whenever I feel lost, in any way, I get back on the computer and share with the sisterhood and almost instantaneously-ping, ping, ping. We are never alone.

We six are really blessed that Karrie intuitively knew that we would make a strong connection with each other. I can't say that we were all in the right place at the right time because of the nature of the catalyst that brought us all together. But in some ways we were meant to be sitting together sharing our tears as well as our laughter. I don't think Karrie ever thought we would continue to be such a strong and important presence in each other's lives and rely so heavily on each other for support more than almost three years later. Only because of Frank's death did I have the opportunity to meet the sisterhood that was created out of such a mélange of pain and sadness. The biggest regret that I had in moving away was being once removed from the personal interaction, like the Friday night dinners and going to places together, but what I did have, even at a distance, continues to be incredibly helpful and supportive.

As I passed the first anniversary of Frank's death, I thought that I would be mysteriously healed, but the opposite happened, I felt worse. I think some of that can be attributed to having unrealistic expectations for the second year. I was also in the let down period, like a postpartum depression, after selling my home, renovating my new apartment, moving, and establishing a new normal-- that new normal keeps raising its ugly head, I still yearn for the old normal. The further I got from the event, the more I was able to view the world with a greater clarity as the fog lifted. I was able to experience life as it really was and would be, and I was trying to keep those demons at bay. I was having trouble sleeping through the night. I still experienced the panic attacks and all the other troublesome symptoms I had experienced during the first year as they continued unabated. As a professional, I understood that I could not heal myself, but could anyone heal me? One early morning as I was lying in bed watching the hands of the clock move slowly from 6:00 a.m. to 6:35 a.m. until I thought it was a reasonable time to get out of bed, I had one of my "aha" moments. I could see that I wasn't making any progress on my own. I was even regressing. I needed some one-on-one help. If nothing else, I did need someone to walk with me on my journey. I also knew that there was no magic person or pill to fix it. I didn't want to keep sharing my pain with others, even close friends and family. I wanted to keep it hidden from others.

I made some calls and ended up finding a psychiatrist who made me feel safe and comfortable. We talked and I cried. Then we talked some more and I cried some more. She prescribed warm baths, massages, meditation, and some medicine, which I didn't want to take. I wanted to heal myself, but I acquiesced and took the pills for a while. It all got me on the right track and helped put my wheels back on. I started to sleep less fitfully at night and I could drive further and further from home without having a panic attack thanks to Bill and his "Safe Driving Course." When I was driving and felt the signs of a panic attack coming on, I would take a deep breath and think of Bill and laugh out loud. I have discovered that I cannot have a panic attack and laugh at the same time.

One day I went to my appointment and was wearing my husband's sweater, his after shower talc, his cologne, and his wedding band. He was particularly fond of Davidoff's "Cool Water" cologne and when he saw it in a store, would buy several bottles as it wasn't always readily available. It had a light, gender neutral scent. When he died he had three bottles in reserve--I guess he thought he was going to live a long time. People's memories of someone are not just visual, but include all the senses, and one of them is sensory. Just feeling his sweater on my skin and smelling his talc and cologne (I became very fond of it) made me feel that Frank was with me. I also sometimes

127

wore his gold wedding band on my middle finger, where it fits along with a few other narrow rings. I really felt embarrassed to tell anyone because I thought they would not understand. That day in the session, I said to the therapist, "Frank is here with me today."

I told her of all the reminders of him that I was wearing. "I am wearing his sweater, his talc, aftershave, and his wedding band."

I asked, "Do you think this a weird thing that I am doing?"

"No, when you don't need to do it anymore, then you won't do it, she responded."

I still wear a light spray of his cologne (I have half a bottle left) I know that when it is finally used up, I won't replace it. No, I still don't share this with anyone else and I do not believe that anyone notices.

THE "NEW NORMAL"

Life is asking me, without much warning, to turn myself inside out and to be a different person. In the first year after Frank had passed away there were moments when I found myself transported out of myself and felt like I belonged in the regular world again. But often it seemed that it was only for a nanosecond because I always get pulled back to the moment of his death. I would see Frank's face and he doesn't look dead; he looks like he is taking a nap (which he was very fond of doing). For a long time, that moment of his death and his face were always there in the upper left hand side of my mind, like on a TV that has a picture in a picture, but I couldn't turn it off, make it smaller, or change the channel. I am not sure I wanted to turn it off because then I might forget him. But the picture has started to fade a little. It is not quite as sharp and fresh as it was when he passed away. However, it is available to conjure up in my mind any time I want to see it, but it doesn't appear so spontaneously these days

I am working on establishing a "new normal," but I realize it is not necessarily a better one. It is not like getting over it, it is more like dealing with the aftermath of a shift in the tectonic plates deep in the ground or ocean before an earthquake. Contrary to what some people may think, it is not possible to go back to normal; in a way it is like starting from ground zero. It is a lot of work, but it is necessary. Having observed other widows, some recently widowed and some widowed for many years, I see how they have dedicated themselves to building a new life even though they may not have called it that. They have filled their lives with many activities, some from their old life and some new to this life including keeping their minds active with book clubs, visits to museums, card games, crossword puzzles, classes, keeping their bodies moving by taking long walks or going to a gym or a yoga class. I can still see the pain and distraction in their eyes. I feel that many widows are just marking time and doing their best, but what they really want is their husbands back with them with all their annoyances and foibles, large or small, even if it is for just one hour or one day.

Six months after Frank died, I sold my home in Water Mill and moved back to the Philadelphia area where I had spent all but the last ten years of my life. During Frank's brief illness, he clearly instructed me to put our home up for sale and move back to the Philadelphia area.

"Deb, go home again," he said.

My children live in Manhattan and Brooklyn and they were encouraging me to move to New York to be nearer to them and my grandchildren. I was very tempted. But I have no history in New York and only one cousin and a few acquaintances in addition to my children and my grandchildren. After giving it much thought and weighing the pros and cons – Philadelphia or New York? I summed up the situation in one sentence, "Nanny doesn't do subways." I already had enough new life skills to learn and riding the New York subway system seemed beyond my abilities. Thirty-five years ago I had mastered the New York subways, but didn't want to do it again. I only went on the subway if I was with my family to serve as my escorts. The alternative to taking a cab or an Uber for any distance was very expensive as I soon learned. One day I took a cab from the upper east side of Manhattan to Park Slope in Brooklyn and it cost $44 and took an hour. The cost and the travel time are the prime reasons people take subways in New York. I couldn't afford to do that very often, I would have to learn to adapt and give up cabs and car services. If I moved to New York, I guess Nanny would have to do subways, like it or not. I opted for the "not."

I settled for Philadelphia where I know the public transportation system and the geography. I thought that Frank's suggestion about moving back to Philadelphia was valid and following that edict was easier than trying to wrestle with the decision by myself. It was as if we made the choice together. Someone bought our house in the Hamptons and I did what Frank had wanted me to do. I know that this is against the rules promulgated by the ever present, "they" who say that one shouldn't make such big decisions for at least a year after the death of a loved one. In hindsight, I think that under the circumstances and with my husband's blessing, I did the right thing for me. I don't see any other decision that I could make better today than I did then regarding my house.

After looking at a lot of apartments and neighborhoods, I made a decision to move to a co-op apartment building, just outside Philadelphia, where I had lived ten years ago. The first time that I came to Philadelphia for a visit and to look at real estate, I visited the same building where I had previously lived. I looked at several apartments that were for sale, and as the elevator arrived at the lobby floor, the doorman who I knew from the time I had lived here before, smiled at me and said, "Welcome home, Mrs. Spungen," Although I had not yet made a decision to buy an apartment, I guess he knew intuitively that I would. And it was like moving home again.

Only after it was a fait accompli, did I realize that my mother had done the very same thing after she was widowed (for the third time). She had been living in St. Thomas in the Virgin Islands for ten years with her husband and then not only moved back to Philadelphia, but to the very same building where she had lived before. I had lived in the Hamptons for ten years and then moved back to the very same building where I had previously lived. Many women have an inexplicable fear of turning into their mothers and there I was becoming my mother by walking almost the identical road that she did. My mother rarely talked to me about her experiences as a widow. I know that she was 27 years old and I was only three months old when her first husband, my father, died at 33 of sepsis. By her demeanor, she passed on to me her strength and resilience in working through her life of being widowed three times. I don't know how she travelled that path with her head held high and a smile on her face. When I was having a particularly bad day handling my grief after Frank's death, I would think of my mother and I would remember how she faced her losses and I learned from the precedents she set. She was my guide.

Many of my neighbors who live in my apartment house were widowed during the time I lived elsewhere and have learned to rely on the other women in the building. They have forged strong relationships in their attempt to find that elusive new normal. Some are old friends from when they were married and some are new friends. They depend on each other for help, support, friendship, and social activities. Almost every day there is a card game in the apartment building's lower level community room. Residents go to the movies and to dinner together, and visit museums. Otherwise many of us would live out our lives alone and isolated from other human beings. Yes, most of the widows have family, children, grandchildren, and even great grandchildren, but they are not always available due to their own busy lives or logistical or geographical constraints. This brings up the issue of being a burden to their families. They all get a lot of joy from their families, but they seem intent on trying not to diminish these relationships by relying on their families too much. They have another family in the apartment building that they can rely on as well.

Often women who are widowed in their 50's and 60's go on to remarry. For the majority of women widowed in their 70's and 80's it is almost too late, but not impossible, to find new male relationships. It is a fact of life that as women age, the available male population dwindles, on-line dating notwithstanding. Initially, as men enter the dating world again in their 70's or 80's, (the majority as a result of being widowed) they seem to be looking for women considerably younger than they are.

From what I have observed, many women who find new relationships with men, whether they marry again or not, often find love or companionship with someone they knew before they were widowed. Perhaps it is a husband of a best friend who has died. It seems easier to be with someone with whom they already feel comfortable than someone new that they have met through introductions by friends (which are few and far between), on-line dating services, etc. I also think the rich widow seems to have an easier time finding meaningful male companionship for obvious and not so obvious reasons. This is not meant as a criticism of anyone's behavior, in fact it is spoken with a modicum of envy. A male friend who used to work in the same office as I did, a long time ago, heard that I was widowed and called me and asked me out for a drink. I went to be social and to see what it would feel like having a date after 54 years. I discovered that he was married and the situation seemed uncomfortable to me and more complicated than what I was prepared for at the time. But I did need to make a different life, like it or not, and have someone to be able to go places such as to movies, restaurants, theater, museums, etc. I needed a new and broader group of friends to share my life, and to allow the aloneness to become more bearable, whether they are male or female friends.

Women of a certain age would welcome male companionship on several levels but have some reluctance to pursue this route as they may have gotten comfortable living alone and not want to live with anyone again. I am beginning to be comfortable with my own company, sometimes I even relish it. They may also be concerned that circumstances might place them in the position of having to take a caregiver role again, especially if they had previously nursed a husband who was in ill health. Other than living with my parents and with my husband, I have never lived by myself. I have started to make my peace with living alone. Sometimes I am very lonely, but I have begun to fill my life with new activities and friends. It is not the same busy as being married, but more like apples and pears. It can be a full life, just a different life. If I keep occupied most of the days and have a few evening activities such as Laughter Yoga, meetings, an occasional movie or other event, out to dinner planned with friends, that works for me. I cannot speak for the future, only for the present. For now, I am OK not having a male friend and maybe OK forever and maybe I don't even have a choice. I would have preferred life as it was, but that life is no longer available to me. I have read that widowers are much more likely to remarry than widows. There is a whole host of reasons for this and needs to be further explored in a wider discussion of gender differences between widows and widowers, but this is not the platform for such a dialogue.

If I were writing this a few years ago, the issue of on-line dating would not have even been mentioned as it didn't exist. It's a whole new dating world, but there are still some choices. If a widow is interested in having a date, there really aren't too many avenues open to her to meet someone. If you are lucky enough to have friends who know a single man they may arrange a "blind date" for you. That doesn't happen too often. Several years after my husband passed away friends arranged a date for me. That was my first blind date since I was 15 years old and that was the only blind date I ever had. I was a little nervous as I walked over to meet "my date" at my friends' apartment. It did feel forcign to me and I didn't know what expectations I ought to have. Once I was there and we all started talking, my apprehension dissipated. We all went to dinner together which I thought made it easier for a first date. I enjoyed being part of a couple at the restaurant and not a fifth wheel. Time and logistics made a second date difficult and my heart didn't sing. A few months after the date, another woman arranged for me to meet a friend of hers. Over a period of a few weeks, we sent emails, and then had some long phone conversations. Finally we met for dinner. It was nice, but the conversation was a little stilted as we tried to find common ground. Both of these dates were fairly recent widowers and seemed to want to talk about their late wives. I listened, and tried to avoid making any comments as I did not want to fall into the role of therapist which as a social worker was tempting to me. I wasn't interested in making my late husband an integral part of the conversation.

A friend of mine, who actually met her future husband on an online dating service, said that she had quite a few dates with men she had met on-line and even if she did not have another date with that person, she usually enjoyed herself. She met interesting people over a cup of coffee or a glass of wine and was not sorry that she had gone on the date. If this is something that intrigues you, then go with it and see where it takes you. It is all part of the new normal.

When I was in the early days of widowhood, I did think often of the dating situation and how I might feel about dating. I thought that maybe this was something I would consider in the future. I was feeling some pressure, maybe it was really encouragement, from family, friends, even my therapist to date. I was often asked questions like, "Are you seeing anyone? Have you thought of on-line dating?" Maybe family and friends don't want me to be lonely and want me to have someone to go out with to the movies or dinner. I can't say that I wasn't tempted, but as time passed I began to feel that this was not a necessity for me in order to live a fuller life. I questioned whether in order to have this new life, I had to have a relationship with a man, whether I couldn't be content without dating. I must admit that I don't try too hard to find a man, Seems too much like work. It isn't that I sit home alone night after night and when I am I don't seem to mind that anymore. The dating scene is still a work in progress for me.

The grief and the raw edges associated with the death of a husband are only one part of the spectrum of widowhood. While you are mourning the death, which, on some level, may well be forever, there is also the need to re-invent yourself. To what end? Not only didn't I have a handbook for widowhood I have been approached by a number of acquaintances who seeing my life as a new widow and worrying that this is what the future may hold for them, as well, asked if I could make some suggestions to help them plan for that nebulous time. I had become an expert, in widowhood by sheer happenstance and didn't really deserve that title. To me, this was the hidden part of widowhood. I had no clue about what lay ahead in trying to find a different life. It was like being born again into a very new and foreign world where you even have to learn a new language. It would be good if I could put all I have learned into a handbook, but it would only serve as my personal guide as each person has a different experience especially from the emotional perspective, and it may not be very helpful to others. The contents would have to be skewed towards more practical matters such as checking accounts, credit cards, real estate, etc.

I have noticed that there is an all-important trio of behaviors that strongly affects the emotional and physical life of a single person after their spouse passes away and possibly throughout the remainder of their lives. Yet, very little attention is paid to it by the widow, friends, family, bereavement groups, or health care professionals. Even the widow feels this trio is not to be discussed either because of guilt, feelings of cheating on her late husband, or just plain embarrassment and nobody brings it up in conversation either private or professional. It seems that no one wants to introduce this subject. The first level of the trio is the importance of touch for widows, and includes but is not limited to holding a child's hand, a feeling of a flutter when someone accidentally brushes by you, a furry pet climbing onto one's lap, or the memory of holding the hand of one's spouse. The second level of this trio is intimacy which is initiated by some level of touching or being touched by another person. The third part of the trio is sex. Many widows report that they might want to talk about the trio, but don't want to initiate the conversation with a friend or health care professional. Some widows feel that the subject is fraught with guilt, embarrassment and is too difficult to talk about. More importantly it is one of those topics that simply doesn't occur to people to bring up in conversation. I have a wonderful primary physician and every year before my annual physical he gives me a questionnaire about health issues to complete. One of the sections has to do with whether I am sexually active. Every year I answer the section that mentions sex differently (although my personal circumstances have not changed), including, "Yes, No, or Not Applicable." My doctor never questions me about my answer or opens up a discussion. I leave it to him, but he always skips that question and moves on. I guess it is my call, but I cannot reach out. I never get an opportunity to discuss these issues in a comfortable environment, professional or otherwise. As widows or widowers, we grieve the many different layers of our previous lives with our late partners. The trio of intimacies is rarely discussed, but sexual grief needs to be talked about.

While I was still living in the Hamptons, I was speaking to a neighbor, Sandra, whom I didn't know very well and who was quite insistent that I share with her the information that she needed to know in the event that her husband may pass away before her. Her husband was standing nearby and he seemed pretty healthy to me although maybe she knew something that I didn't know or she just liked to plan ahead. I thought about it and after pondering the question for few minutes, I finally asked her if she had a credit card in her name only and suggested that if she didn't, she should apply for one. After that, my mind drew a blank. Sandra seemed a bit disappointed as I think she expected a lot more information from me. She even took out a piece of paper and a pen from her purse and looked like she was about to take notes. I felt that her question was one of the more unusual questions that I had been asked in the aftermath of Frank's death. She was quite serious about obtaining the information and I seemed to be the best person to give it to her at the moment. Why she anointed me as the widow expert I wasn't quite sure; perhaps I just looked like a like a capable widow, although I had only been widowed for a few months.

One of the difficulties in finding a new normal is establishing relationships with other women whom you could count on to be available for various activities such as, dinner, movies, travel, etc. One of the reasons I moved from the Hamptons was that there weren't many single women, widowed or divorced, at least that I knew. The few I met, other than my support group friends and a handful of other close neighbors and friends, seemed to have their own clique and didn't seem very welcoming to admitting new women to their club. It made me think of the movie "Mean Girls." I am not sure what was required of me to apply for membership. A single woman I knew, upon hearing that Frank had passed away, offered to exchange phone numbers with me and promised that she would call and we would get together. Two months passed and I did not hear from her. I had two tickets to a show (that I had bought before Frank had gotten sick) so I called and invited her to go with me. She replied that she was busy and that she would call me soon and make a date to do something together. I felt like she had brushed me off, as I never heard from her again. It was very disappointing, even hurtful, like being a teenager again and a boy said he would call you and he didn't. The evening before I moved I was with my daughter and saw this woman and her friends at the movies. We exchanged greetings. I told her that I was moving the very next day and she seemed surprised. I think that I gave her a greeting that was less than pleasant, but I felt upset with her because in the six months since my husband died she had made no attempt to contact me. I am sure that she has a busy life and did not seem to have time to let me into it. On the other hand, when I offered the tickets to my neighbor who had been kindly feeding me dinner on a weekly basis, she volunteered her husband to stay home and Carolyn made it a ladies night out and we went to dinner and a show. It was my first foray into what could be thought of as a social evening. I can say that it was enjoyable although it left me with a slightly off kilter feeling as it was such a different experience. I hope there is a lesson in this for me. When I have friends or acquaintances who find themselves suddenly single, I will reach out to them and offer to include them in things that I do. I think we should all make an effort to do so.

It seemed like a lot of work to make new friends, and I wasn't very successful at it at first. I hoped it would be different in Philadelphia. All of my schooling, from pre-school through college and graduate school, was in Philadelphia and the surrounding area. I also had some family in Philadelphia. This seemed a propitious beginning in my attempt to find a new life. The first day I was back in the area, I went out to lunch by myself at a delicatessen near my apartment. As I headed to my table, I heard the name, "Debbie." (I used to be called "Debbie" a lot when I was younger) ricocheting around the room. There were five or six women sitting there eating lunch, some of whom I had spent the three years of high school eating at the very same lunch period.

"You are back!" they all exclaimed in a chorus as they hugged and kissed me.

"How wonderful was that?"

The advice that I have consistently gotten from other widows was that I should try to make an effort to meet new women and with whom I had some interests in common. It was akin to making friends when you moved to a new school. In Philadelphia, many of my close women friends were part of a couple and they included me in activities, both alone and with their spouses and we all felt comfortable doing that.

My friend, Susan, has been divorced for many years, and we have been friends almost since the day we were born (I am older by 17 days). We lived next door to each other and were in the same room from nursery school through high school. We even had our Sweet Sixteen party together. Our parents were good friends as well. When I moved away, we stayed in touch, but did not see each other very much. As soon as I moved back, she took me under her wing and our friendship picked up where we had left off. After I moved back to Philadelphia, the first time we were together, she hugged me and said, "And I am glad that you're home."

Over the years, Susan had built a full life and had made lots of female friends, but our relationship is special. We don't include each other in all our activities because although we enjoy each other's company we have different interests, too. We are always there for each other. We talk on the phone and email several times a day almost like when we were teenagers (except now we are in the computer generation). She plays a lot of card games like canasta and bridge. I now feel that I was amiss in not learning how to play bridge. I could never seem to find the time to learn the game. I was amazed to find out how many women, single or married, play Bridge, Mah Jong, or Canasta, but bridge seems to be the game of choice among older women. Someone told me that when you are young, bridge is entertainment, when you are older, bridge is a necessity. I didn't know that 35 years ago that I would be a widow and that playing bridge could be an important part of my social life and good for stimulating the brain. I understand that now, but I think it may be too late for me to learn the game, but I may still give it a try. When I was in Florida, I discovered that they were giving free Mah Jong lessons at my resort. I took quite a few lessons, and although I thought it was challenging, it was fun and I met some very nice new people. When I came home I did not start to play, but I am thinking about it. Games seem to be a fun activity and they are a wonderful way to pass the time. Solitaire doesn't count, consider the name of the game.

MOVING ON

The question of moving to a new home comes up frequently in the immediacy after the death of a partner. There are a variety of choices;

1. Move
2. Don't move
3. Rent
4. Buy
5. None of the above

There is no right or wrong answer to the puzzle. No matter how much you examine the conundrum what to do continues to elude you. You think you have come to a conclusion and the next day you wake up and it has fallen apart again. Family and friends try to help by jumping in with advice which only serves to muddy the waters. If you could only see the issue in hindsight it might help, but that is not doable. Having some understanding of why you have imposed such a weighty problem on yourself can help in sorting the problem out. For some, it may be a financial issue, for others it may have to do with the loss you have just sustained. If you move into a new home, and it doesn't work out, you always have the opportunity to change what you have done at some time in the future. There is always a Plan B to your Plan A. When I sold my house in the Hamptons and moved back to an apartment in the Philadelphia area, I must admit to second guessing my decision for a while, but I thought I would just see how it all played out. I am more than pleased with the quality of my new life here. No matter how much I search for Frank he is not in my new home. I miss his presence terribly I know that he is with me. This is fine for me, for others it may not be helpful. I enjoy all aspects of living in my apartment. Even though Frank had never lived here, I still feel his presence. I am surrounded by my many cherished belongings that Frank and I collected over the years. It didn't happen overnight, but the comfort level slowly increased and I began to feel more peaceful because this is my home now. No more second thoughts. On an emotional level I feel safe here. This is one more issue that I did not have to deal with any longer.

Frank's prognostication was correct. On December 30, 2010, almost six months after his death, I had closing on the house. The road to that event had not been easy or straight forward, but the end result was the desired one. First a buyer made an offer and after some negotiations we agreed on a price. Was it the price I wanted? No, but it seemed to be the right thing to do for me and not sit there and wait for a better offer as the bills kept piling up. Everything seemed to be moving along, the inspection had been done, lawyers hired, and papers drawn up, and then the buyer dropped out when he split with his girlfriend. Two months later he came back, with no girlfriend, an all-cash deal, and he wanted closing within six weeks. This is what I wanted, but the reality of it was not easy to assimilate. I had lived here with my husband for almost 11 years and we had loved our home, with its flower gardens, peach trees, and beautiful bucolic

146

views. Our life was everything we hoped it to be in this lovely and peaceful home. Our daughter and son-in-law had a home nearby and our son and his wife and their children, our grandchildren, came out often to visit. We had special family times together here.

Selling the house was a first step in my new life. Remaining in the Hamptons, beyond my husband's clear directive was really not a good idea, but when the deal was done, I found myself very conflicted even though I knew that this was a necessary step for a number of reasons; the house was too large for me to live there by myself (I was only using the country kitchen, the bathroom, and my bedroom) The maintenance was like a full time job, and much too expensive, and it was a more isolating life than I wanted. The job that I had ahead of me, to pack up and move out within a six-week period, was daunting. Even if I had been given more time to do what had to be done, I don't think it would have been any easier. In some ways, I think that this was the better way, get it over and done with as quickly as possible and not belabor the associated angst. That part of my life was finished, too prematurely I thought, and I had to shut the door on it, except for the good memories. Frank had died there, and I felt a little guilty "leaving" him there, at least his spirit, and I hoped he would go with me.

As they say in text messages, "OMG," how would I ever be able to do this by myself? The house had lots of storage space and we filled it all up. I never envisioned having to do this job alone. I thought

147

Frank would be there to help. I had started this sorting about six weeks after Frank had passed away, knowing that moving out of the house was coming sooner than later. A dear friend Judy from Philadelphia offered to come up to the Hamptons and help me clean out Frank's office, since his one man business had ceased to exist the day he died. Judy was fast, well-organized, and very strong, a lot like the Energizer Bunny, a good friend to have. Judy did most of the work and I only had to direct her and answer questions about what papers needed to be kept or what to throw out. We also sorted out the many books as I had arranged to give them to a non-profit group to distribute to libraries and sell the remainder in their thrift shop. The job was finished in one day! Judy was planning to stay for three days so she asked, "I have two more days. What else do you want me to do? You have my undivided time so take advantage of me."

I thought for a moment and decided that we should sort out Frank's clothes. It would be easier with someone there to help me. I might as well get to the job. There was no pressure for me to do this. Many widows don't do this for months or years; it is a very personal issue there is no right or wrong time. It just felt right for me to do it now. It is not an easy task. I hadn't really given it any thought before this, just knowing that I would have to do it sometime in the future. I thought, since I had Judy to help, "Let's get it done" and so we started the next morning. I called the charitable organization that was coming for the books and I asked if they also picked up used clothing. They told us how to pack the clothing in big trash bags, (that felt sad). I had been advised by a number of family and friends that I should carefully look through all the pockets before giving the clothing away as people often left important items in their pockets as well as money. I felt like I was intruding into Frank's personal space, but we did it.

Every time I thought we were finished, I found another drawer or closet area filled with more clothing. Frank had more clothes and socks and underwear than I could ever have imagined. Whenever he bought something new, he never gave away the old things, but quietly packed them away to be used, when? I guess the answer to that question is "Never." As we took the clothes out of the dresser drawers and off the hangers in his closet, we did a thorough check of all of his pockets. This is a list of what we found: 10 packets of travel size tissues, seventeen cents, and a gold filling that the dentist must have given him when he had to have a tooth pulled the year before. Judy later sold the filling for $35.00 to a jeweler who bought gold. The treasure hunt was for naught.

That job completed, now I had to examine all my options for getting the remainder of the house sorted and packed up. My children could only come on the weekends to help but I needed more than two weekends to do the job. Family and friends are helpful, but most of them lived in Philadelphia and even then, at our age, friends come and after one or two hours their back or knees hurt and they can't do anymore and then you still need to reciprocate when they move. I

149

didn't have too many "Judy's." My daughter saved the day with a suggestion that I hire two women she knew who had a business that specialized in organizing people's moves, homes, closets, offices, stuff or whatever else needs organizing. I had to pay them for their work, but Stacy and Sarah did what a room full of friends could never do even if we had more time and were a lot younger. Another plus being that Stacy and Sarah were completely objective about all the items in my home. If it is financially and logistically possible, I would highly recommend engaging a professional organizer to help with a move. It definitely lowers the stress level. They came from New York City to my home in Water Mill and helped me orchestrate my move. Having someone objectively organize your life is a real boon. I was moving from a small four bedroom house to a two bedroom apartment in the Philadelphia suburbs, and there were many things that I did not or could not to take with me.

It was a fairly complex move; some items went to the estate sale (AKA garage sale), some went into storage, summer clothes and other items that I would need in my apartment in Florida were going with me, winter clothes that I would need when I returned from Florida in early March, personal papers, my computer and printer, and, most importantly, my papers to prepare my tax returns when I got back. All the items not going to be sold or moved into storage were to be packed in my car and taken to a friend's house until my return, while the rest went into my car to be driven to Florida. I am a list maker and so I had many lists all over the place including post-it notes pasted up and down my arms. In addition, the organizer ladies made backup computer lists and not one item ended up going to the wrong place. The logistics were almost more complicated than moving an entire army battalion. Just reading this makes me feel anxious again. I think that any move has its elements of chaos, but it was really necessary to keep it all under control. Stacy and Sarah had no emotional agenda or vested interest in my stuff. They could afford to be objective in helping me make decisions about whether or not I should keep, give away, or sell my stuff. They were very professional, but also calm and gentle in their affect, very Zen-like, and I never felt pressured to make a decision. The plan was for the organizers (I called them "my ladies") to pre-pack items to get them ready for the movers as well as preparing for the three day house sale and keeping the different parts of the move segregated. They worked all day and left for the night planning to return the next day to finish the job. Everything seemed to be working well in what was close to a perfect plan in preparation for an almost pain-free moving, but there was a searing emotional pain in seeing my home, my things, and my life deconstructed in front of my eyes. Soon it no longer felt like my home. This was when the wheels started to come off and my sadness increased exponentially. This process was really difficult. I guess that should not be a surprise.

WHERE IS THE TOOTH FAIRY?

Sarah and Stacy left at the end of the first day to stay with friends. I was hungry for dinner, but I think I was even more tired than hungry. I didn't want to go out for dinner and I realized that there was almost no food left in the house. I rummaged around in the freezer and found a few frozen cookies. I bit into a still frozen chocolate chip cookie with walnuts, certainly not a good choice for dinner. Unfortunately, I felt something crunch, not the nut in the cookie, but the root of one of my back molars. The tooth had been extremely sensitive for the last few weeks, but the dentist said he couldn't find anything wrong.

I looked in the mirror and saw one of those creatures from a vampire movie. Part of the tooth was still firmly attached in the gum, but a long piece had separated from the main part and was swinging freely and it hurt. I called the dentist and he said to come into his office at 8:00 a.m. the next morning and to take something for the pain. I took two Extra Strength Tylenol and went to bed.

One dentist looked at the tooth, and then the senior partner looked at it. The root was cracked, but the consensus was that the tooth might be saved. I would have to go through several root canal procedures before we knew that saving the tooth was even possible. The question then became when could I do that since I was moving in less than a week and every day I was fully involved with the process.

I had had the same problem with another fractured molar a few years ago, and after several root canal procedures, the tooth could not be saved and had to be pulled. I had also developed a terrible infection and the strong doses of antibiotics that I had to take had given me a severe bacterial infection (C-Diff Bacterial Colitis) which made me quite ill for months. To me, a tooth is a tooth and not a living thing. I made a decision, based on what happened the last time I tried to save a tooth and the timing of this event, that it needed to be pulled, and my dentist concurred. It was a "perfect storm" in the dentistry world (a portent of what was to come) leaving me with no viable alternatives.

My dentist did not perform extractions so he sent me to a dental surgeon. I made the appointment for the extraction, but was told that the dentist had to see me first to try to talk me out of pulling the tooth. He could not see me until the next day. When I got to the dentist, he gave me a hard time because he thought he could save the tooth.

He just didn't get my situation at all. His receptionist didn't like me when I said, "A tooth is not a living thing." She told me that it was. My decision prevailed, after all the tooth was in my mouth, and I made an appointment for the extraction the next day. I had to arrange for someone to drive me to the dentist and someone else to drive me home. I was feeling very alone and sorry for myself because, for the first time I was going to have to rely on others to help me and not my husband who would have driven me and sat patiently in the waiting room doing crossword puzzles. The extraction went fine and wasn't terribly painful, but I was feeling a different kind of pain. The person who drove me home, just walked me to the door, asked, "Are you OK?" I nodded and they went on their way. And there I was, like it or not. Ricky Ricardo wasn't waiting for me when I entered the house. I was supposed to put ice off and on my cheek every 20 minutes for the entire night. I also had to bite down on those weird little cotton rolls that resembled white Tootsie Roll Juniors to help staunch the bleeding. I have a bleeding disorder and had already had an infusion of a blood property to keep me from bleeding excessively. It was a terrible night, probably one of the worst ones I have ever spent, and I was so alone. I don't usually consider myself a pathetic person, but this was beyond the pale. I don't remember ever feeling so pitiful in my entire life as I did that night and that was not an exaggeration of my plight. I wondered, "How I am supposed to sleep if I have to go down to the kitchen every twenty minutes to get fresh ice and then when I take it off for 20 minutes how would I be able to wake up again in 20 minutes to reapply the ice?"

I couldn't find my ice pack as it was already in a carton for moving, and I did not feel well enough to go to the drugstore and buy another one. I had heard that a bag of frozen peas makes an excellent ice pack (I was admonished to keep the peas in the bag), and I found a bag of peas in the freezer and used them. It worked quite well, but by the time the 20 minute session was up, they were starting to defrost and although I popped them back in the freezer for 20 more minutes, they were not quite frozen again at the end of the next 20 minutes. I looked around in the freezer and I found a bag of wild blueberries. Nobody had ever mentioned frozen blueberries as a substitute for an ice pack, but they seemed to fill the bill as well as peas. I alternated the peas and the blueberries off and on every 20 minutes all night so they could have time to refreeze. I managed to rouse myself every 20 minutes and to go downstairs to the freezer. I was feeling exhausted and overwhelmed. I was really getting a taste of what "aloneness" meant.

I had never been through any kind of illness before without my husband there to help me. My level of pathetic grew with each trip up and down the stairs. The bleeding from my gum continued and exacerbated, and the dentist had not given me enough of those cotton rolls. I was uneasy (to put it mildly) about the bleeding. Although I had been pretreated, this seemed to me to be excessive bleeding. I tried to think of what I could use as a substitute for the cotton rolls, something absorbent and more or less sterile – cotton balls wouldn't do it. I thought maybe tampons or sanitary pads, but I didn't have any. Every time I drifted off into an uneasy sleep and woke up (with the assist of the alarm set at 20 minute intervals), I had all this bloody drool dripping down my chin onto my pillow. No matter how much I wished my husband could be by my side, I knew that wasn't going to happen.

I wondered if there was such a thing as a "Rent a Husband" agency or maybe it was something I could create for other widows who find themselves in a similar situation. It would be akin to a male "Mary Poppins" arriving in a shower of stars and exiting in the same manner through the chimney, negating my having to get out of bed and go downstairs to open the door. It sounds other worldly, but it was a nice thought to keep close to me. That night, I didn't need a nurse or any other kind of companion or caretaker, just a husband "To soothe my fevered brow" or to ask, "Do you need your bag of peas?" or to say "Let me wipe the drool for you," or "Is there anything else I can get for you?" or just be there by my side. We didn't need to like each other, and emotions would play no part in this arrangement as it would be strictly a professional service. In the morning, I would pay his hourly fee with my credit card (and I wouldn't have to say "thank you" or "I am sorry to have kept you up all night") and he could go on to his next job. The "Rent a Husband" would not be an ideal situation, but it would sure beat being alone. Finally that long night ended. The bleeding had stopped as I remembered around 5:00 a.m. that one of the remedies used to stop bleeding after a tooth extraction was to bite down on a tea bag that has been first soaked in hot water. The tannic acid in the tea helps to make the blood clot. The moral to this story is, no matter how hungry or stressed out, don't eat frozen chocolate chip cookies with nuts straight out of the freezer. Frozen cake, without nuts, is a safer bet.

I did not get much sleep that night, but in the morning I had surprisingly little swelling, probably due to my compliant use of the ice packs (frozen peas and wild blueberries), but I didn't feel very well—like I had been run over by a truck. I wanted to stay in bed for the day, but that was not to be. By 9:00 a.m., the two organizers arrived for the second day of work as well as the three people who were going to tag the articles for the house sale for items that I was not taking with me to Philadelphia. Each group was constantly calling me to come and look at things as there was a lot of decision making to be done on my part. Every time I moved from one staging area to another, I had to sit down as I was completely exhausted and out of it. I couldn't even make it up the stairs without stopping to rest. In hindsight, I realized that I may have made some wrong decisions about what to take and what to sell, but it couldn't be helped. My thought processes were not firing on all cylinders; some were still asleep numbed by my physical and emotional pain. In my own work, I often told people who were going through the aftermath of the violent death of a family member or friend not to be too hard on themselves. I had to remember to apply that admonition to myself as well. I was a little disappointed that after all that pain when I looked under my pillow in the morning, the tooth fairy had not even visited me. I realized that I had forgotten to leave the tooth under the pillow as the dentist had thrown it away without asking me if I wanted it.

SELLING STUFF

Having a tag, garage, or estate sale is a good way to winnow down your "stuff" when you are moving and can't take it all with you, and maybe want to make some extra money. It is possible to do it yourself, but it is a very difficult and time consuming job as everything has to be separated into "Sell" and "Don't Sell" category. There are also other details like managing the sale so people don't walk off with things without paying for them. Some of the buyers are pretty slick grabbing things off of walls and tables. And I found that some people will buy anything, even a broken dust pan. Although I did make some money at the end of the three days, I wouldn't call it fun, maybe more of a learning experience. I hope there is no next time, but if there is, I would do it differently.

Although I have done a sale with my husband before, I clearly could not do it myself this time due to the circumstances and also there were more items to sell. From the time that I signed the sales contract until moving day I only had five weeks. The only available weekend for the sale was the one before Christmas. I wondered, "Is this a good time to have a sale so close to Christmas?" I had no choice as I had run out of weekends. As it turned out it was a very good weekend for an estate sale. I hired a company to handle the process. It was owned by two business partners, and I am not sure what other relationships they shared. For my purposes, I will call them Dick and Jane. Jane was very sharp and Dick, that's another story. There was no question who was in charge of this operation. Dick had a truck so if people bought large or heavy items, he delivered them (for a fee) to the buyer's house. Dick and Jane specialized in estate sales and took care of the myriad of details involved in such an undertaking, like tagging the items, putting advertisements in the newspapers, and handling all the details of the sale. They had been recommended to me ostensibly by a happy customer, who I think may have secretly been Dick and Jane's cousin and who did not tell the truth. I would not recommend them to anyone else for reasons I shall explain shortly.

Dick and Jane suggested that the sale should run for three days. Friday through Sunday. Dick, Jane, and Jane's grown son came and tagged for two days in preparation for the sale. They moved things around so that items for sale were grouped together, such as dishes, drinking glasses, etc. This also allowed for parts of the house to be blocked off to keep people out of areas where nothing was for sale, such as my bedroom, or the buyers would have snatched up those items as well. It was suggested that I be out of the house during the actual sale, as it was easier for the owner not to see people buying their stuff to which they are emotionally attached. At the time it sounded like a good plan. It was not a good idea, as I was soon to discover. I think that Dick and Jane just wanted me out of the way so they could run the sale the way they wanted to without any interference from the owner, me.

159

Even though I thought that the weekend before Christmas might not be a good one for a sale, I was wrong as evidenced by the long line of people snaking up my driveway at 8:00 a.m., over an hour before the sale was to begin. I think there was a lot of Christmas shopping going on. I had made plans to go out to do some errands, have lunch with a friend, and then hide out in another friend's house for a few hours.

I was still recovering from my tooth fiasco and was physically and emotionally drained, so I decided to go home around 3:00 p.m. so that I could rest for a little while. The door to the bedroom had tape across it that said "Do Not Enter-Owner Inside." The yellow tape reminded me of police tape. When I got home people were all over the house. Jane was seated at a card table near the front door so that people had to go by her to exit the house, thereby, hopefully, paying for the items they were carting out the door. I wondered who was guarding (and I discovered that is the operative word here) the other two exits. I poked my head into the garage and I was just in time as Dick was helping someone, ostensibly a customer, (not his relative) remove my back-up refrigerator from the garage, which I was leaving for the new owner. They were halfway to the opened garage door.

"Where are you going with the refrigerator?"

"This man bought it and I am helping him take it to his truck," Dick said.

"No, you are not. I never said it was for sale."

He glared at me and put it back in place. I began to realize that tagged or not, apparently everything was for sale or maybe there for the taking. There was not much I could do. I couldn't stop the sale. We still had two days to go, and I couldn't handle the rest of it myself. I am not sure if it just got out of control, and they didn't have enough eyes to watch everything and/or there was some hanky panky going on. I will never know. Some of the shrinkage can be attributed to the overzealous buyers. Many of them tried to buy anything or everything, even if it was not tagged or broken. They acted like a swarm of locusts. It was a little scary, the average person at their worst.

Day one was just about over as Dick and Jane closed down promptly at 5:00 p.m. Months after I had moved, I would realize that I couldn't find some items that must have been sold or walked away, but were definitely not tagged for sale. Nothing terribly expensive, but items like Frank's big Scrabble game, videos, my grabber, etc. They and many other items remain MIA. On day two, I made a decision to stay in the house for most of the day and keep my eye on things even though I don't think that Dick and Jane were too happy about it. I stayed in my room for brief periods and no one tried to enter maybe because I had taped an additional sign on my door, "Large dog in there with owner, too." Occasionally I would come out and wander around and try to keep an eye on things.

When Day Two ended at 5:00 p.m. Dick and Jane were out the door so fast I could hardly see them disappear down the driveway and into their car. I collapsed on the sofa and tried to catch my breath. I looked around at my totally deconstructed home. I almost didn't recognize it. With much of the furniture and personal belongings gone, the house had an uncomfortable echo. About an hour later, I was still sitting on the sofa too tired to move when the doorbell rang. I looked out the window and I recognized a nice looking man who had been at the house earlier in the day and had bought two white Adirondack chairs. He had shown some interest in the breakfront in the living room and said, "I would like to bring my wife back later to look at it. It would be perfect in our new kitchen."

He didn't clarify what "later" meant. He was quite tall and had a big head of blond hair that kept flopping over his forehead. Accompanying him was a very tall, attractive, blond woman whom he introduced as his wife. A large white, new model, open back pick-up truck was also parked in my driveway. He seemed harmless enough so I opened the door a crack.

"We are closed for the day, and you will have to come back tomorrow."

He responded rather forcefully and spoke rapidly as if he were used to being in charge.

"My name is John Flynn and this is my wife, Valerie, we are both lawyers from Southampton. I have to take an early train tomorrow morning to go into New York City and I want to show my wife the breakfront in the living room."

I was not sure where he lived or what his profession was had anything to do with it, but I guess he thought it would give him some credibility. He seemed like a person who would bully people into getting whatever he wanted. I told him that I would have to call Dick and Jane and see if they could come back.

"Hi, Jane, the man that bought the white chairs earlier today has returned with his wife to show her the piece of furniture in the living room and wants to see it now."

"We're tired and we're eating dinner – just tell him to come back tomorrow and don't let him in. You are in that house all by yourself and it isn't safe."

"I am sorry Mr. Flynn, they can't come back tonight. You will have to come back tomorrow or just skip it."

With that, he pushed open the door and barged in with his wife close behind him as if I had not even spoken to him. He strode over to the breakfront to show it to his wife. Not only was he a bully, but his affect seemed a little manic to me. I wasn't afraid of him. I just wanted him to leave, but he made it pretty clear that he wouldn't without taking the breakfront with him.

"We will take it, here's the money."

He handed me a wad of rolled up bills, which I stuck in my pocket without counting it as we had set the price for the furniture when he was here earlier.

"Call me John," he said as if he were my new best friend.

"When are you coming back for it?" I asked.

"I am going to take it right now. Do you have any tools?"

The breakfront had to be dismantled as it was custom made and installed as two separate pieces because the doorway in the room was too narrow for a larger piece of furniture to make the turn out to the front door.

"I have no idea where the tools might be, either sold or packed. Please leave now," I said,

He acted as if he hadn't heard me or didn't care.

"Do you have a knife?"

"A knife?"

This was getting a little out of control for me.

"What kind of knife and what for?"

"I need a dinner knife to take it apart."

Now this was going from scary to weird. It was as if everyone took furniture apart with a table knife. It was now 7:30 p.m. I was exhausted, hungry and my jaw ached. I sat down on the one remaining piece of furniture in the room, a sofa, to watch the John Flynn show, "Dismantling the Breakfront with a Bread Knife." I went into the kitchen and found a dinner knife which fortunately or unfortunately hadn't been packed. While I was doing that, John ran out to the truck (he moved quickly at whatever he was doing) to get some quilted movers' blankets and carefully spread them on the floor and created a covered pathway to the front door. This showed me that he had every confidence that he would be able to disassemble and remove the breakfront. He took the knife and began dismantling the breakfront and giving his wife directions on how to assist him.

The knife flashed back and forth at breakneck speed. He looked like the knife thrower in the circus except he was using a dull table knife. I didn't know if he knew what he was doing or he was making it up as he went along. Soon the heavy glass doors were removed, wrapped in additional movers' blankets and taken out to the truck. John separated the top section of the breakfront from the bottom and he and Valerie carried it out to the truck. It was very heavy and I don't know how the two of them were able to accomplish the job. I was sure that this was a first, the use of a table knife to dismantle a huge piece of furniture, and without damaging the furniture or the knife. Maybe John was practicing for an upcoming audition for "This Old House" television show on PBS. It was a peculiar demonstration of a 100 ways to use a table knife.

After the top part of the breakfront was separated and removed, he started on the bottom. He began to pull it away from the wall, but he soon realized that it was somehow tethered to the wall by electrical wires and with very little play in the connection. The furniture had been there for almost eight years and I had forgotten how it had been installed. The tether was a bundle of electric wires that went from an opening in the back wall of the unit to a hole in the dry wall and was connected to the electrical box in the basement instead of an electric plug. The wires were from the sound system which seemed rather elaborate, at least it was to me.

"I have to cut the wires and tie them off. Do you have a special kind of electrical pliers that I could use that would cut the wires and seal the ends?" John asked.

I had no idea what he was talking about, and no, I didn't have any pliers anyway. Apparently the table knife would not solve this issue. John looked a little perplexed as he scratched his head searching for a solution. But he would not be deterred from his goal for long, his mind moved too quickly.

"Where's the breaker box? I want to see if I can find the breaker for the stereo wires and then I can turn the breaker off until I can cut the wires somehow. Otherwise when I cut them, the wires will be live."

I was now really frightened by the antics of this mad man. John was probably more strange than mad, but at the time, I found dealing with him more than a little off-putting.

"Please leave now. Tomorrow I will get the electrician to come over and disconnect the wires properly," I said.

He ignored me and went to the basement and switched all the breakers off and on, causing the lights in the house to flicker off and on, as the breakers weren't all tagged properly and he never found the right one.

I kept repeating, "Please go now, this is too dangerous." I was envisioning that the house would catch fire and burn down two days before closing--not a good thought. Back up from the basement he came. It was getting later and later, it was already past 9:00 p.m.

"Do you have scissors?" he asked.

"I just have small toe nail scissors in my cosmetic bag."

"I think that will do. I have had big electrical shocks before, I can handle it."

"I think you should leave now," I kept repeating like a newly found mantra, but to no avail.

He never even paused for a moment to consider my command, at least I thought it was a command. I guess John only thought it was a mild suggestion.

When he cut the wires, not much happened, it was a little anti-climactic. John didn't seem to even get a mild shock. I must admit that I was a little disappointed, I half expected him to go down (or is it up?) in flames. He just kept moving briskly along with the toe nail scissors and the dinner knife. Much to my chagrin, after he pulled the bottom of the breakfront away from the wall, I discovered several large holes in the drywall where the wires were pulled through and holes in the back of the furniture where the wires protruded. John didn't seem to mind the holes in the furniture as he said they wouldn't show when he placed it against the wall in his kitchen. The holes in the wall were my problem and I would be in big trouble if I couldn't get someone to come over the next day to fix the wall and paint it as it was almost "D-Day"; two more days to closing on the house.

Around 10:00 p.m., John had completed the job and he and Valerie dragged and slid the bottom portion of the piece out and up on the truck bed, wrapping it with the movers' quilts. He secured it all with bungee straps as part of the furniture was too long for the truck bed and it was hanging over the rear deck of the truck. John returned my trusty "tools" to me, bid me goodbye, and climbed into the cab of the truck with Valerie. Off they sped into the dark cold night never to be heard from or seen again. That left me with my mouth agape and an amazed look on my face as I still couldn't comprehend how he could have dismantled such a large and complicated piece of furniture with only a kitchen knife. I dragged myself up to my bed.

The next day, I counted the money that I had put in my pocket and realized that he had short changed me on the amount that we had agreed upon. At the very least he could have called or texted me to say how nice the breakfront looked installed in their new kitchen. I guess John was concerned that I would ask him for the balance of the money. What an end to such a dramatic episode. I did find a contractor that had previously worked for me, and out of sheer kindness, sent one of his workers over immediately to fix and paint the wall. In terms of all of the chaos of that last week in my home, that included the tooth extraction, the organizing of my belongings, the estate sale, the one event that I most clearly remember is the John Flynn episode. In hindsight it gives me a good laugh.

Some things that I sold, I am sorry now that I did. I have been looking for them ever since. Selling some other things, made me feel freer, less encumbered. Over the years, we had collected a lot of lovely items such as paintings, ceramics, hand blown glass and other object d'art that Frank and I bought together on trips and at museum craft shows. My first thought was to part with all of my collections and art, selling the better items at a consignment shop or to an art auction house, not so much for the profit that I might realize from the sale, but also to make my new apartment more minimalist (whatever that means). But then I realized that they were all part of my life with my husband and each and every item had a back story and a lovely memory attached to it. I planned my apartment so I could display most of the items and hang almost all of my art and now I am happily surrounded by all the things I love. It gives my home its unique personality and keeps my husband with me. I am really pleased that I kept most of my treasures.

MOVING DAY—PART 1

The next week was the week before Christmas and I seem to have no memory of it at all except going to the dentist to have my dental surgery checked out. I assume I spent the time finishing up the packing and organizing to get ready for the movers who were due the Monday after Christmas. The move was planned to take place over a two day period, Monday and Tuesday. The first day the movers would pack everything and the second day the movers would load everything on the truck. The cleaning people would follow the movers from room to room cleaning the house to make it ready for the new owner's walk through before closing on the property. Over the last few weeks, when asked when I was moving, I answered, "Monday, December 27th, the day of the big blizzard," which was meant as a joke because it was exactly what I didn't want to happen.

Even if you don't remember the date, I think you can guess the punch line of this story. On Saturday, Christmas Day, the weather forecasters started to predict a heavy snow storm to start by mid-day Sunday. The weather on Christmas day was cold, but clear, with a startling cloudless blue sky, and I tried to believe that the weather forecasters were going to be wrong. They were wrong, but they erred in the other direction. This was not to be just an ordinary snowfall, but a real blizzard with snowfall totals from 25" to 30" not including the drifts. High winds were expected to accompany the snow. The Hamptons area doesn't usually get such big snow falls because of the more temperate climate, with the Atlantic Ocean on the south shore and Long Island Sound on the north. I had high hopes that this quirk in the weather would continue to bode well and keep the intensity of the storm more inland towards New York City. Long Island has a TV channel which repeats the weather forecast and traffic report on a loop, three minutes for each with a commercial in-between. I still had one TV connected and I became obsessed with watching the weather forecast, thinking if I watched it incessantly I could magically control it. Unfortunately, the more I watched it, the worse the forecast became. On Sunday, just as predicted, the snow started to fall heavily by midday and continued all night and into the next morning. I kept calling the snow plow company, to come and clear my driveway as I still believed that the movers would arrive on Monday morning to do the packing. The snow plow company didn't want to come and plow until the snow stopped because they didn't want to come by for a second pass at the driveway. But they finally made it to my house about 4:00 a.m., although the snow had not yet stopped, the intensity had slowed down somewhat. By then, there was an accumulation of more than 25" of snow on the ground, and snow drifts added to that total, with more to come. The movers called about 7:00 a.m. to tell me that they couldn't make it to my house, and the move would have to be postponed until the next day. They promised that they would bring an extra crew of movers and would stay as long as necessary until they had packed and loaded all of my belongings and get it all done in one day. My anxiety level was pretty high by then, I was helpless, I had no choice.

I lived on the eastern end of Long Island and the movers were based in Long Island City, almost two hours away under normal driving conditions. There was nothing I could do, but wait it out until Tuesday and trust the movers' word. As promised, they did make it out to my house very early the next day. They closed the door on the moving truck, and the cleaning crew followed them out the door at exactly 9:00 p.m. Even though I had sold a lot of furniture, my things still filled the truck. It was done. Ten years of my life were packed up, and I only had my memories that would always be with me. I knew that moving away would not heal me, but it was a way to start over. The house looked so neat and clean, but without any life in it, as it had looked the first day we had moved in. No one was left in the house but my daughter and me. I knew I was going to lose it. I started to weep for all the wonderful times there and for what would never be again. I turned and walked out for the very last time.

I thought that chapter in my life was almost complete or as complete as it would ever be. But it wasn't quite that easy. As I left my house and walked slowly to my car, my legs felt very heavy, like they were stuck in quicksand. I finally got to my car and headed over to my daughter's mother-in-law's house where I was going to stay for the next two days until the real estate closing of my house. Everywhere I looked the snow was still piled up all over the roads. I pulled into her driveway and immediately got hung up on the drifts with all four wheels spinning in the air as the bottom of the car rested on what looked like a mountain of snow. For years, I had driven an SUV and

173

never had a problem driving it in the snow. My new car was a sedan with only front wheel drive and sat much lower than an SUV (especially one that was fully packed with my belongings for my trip to Philadelphia). It was my first experience of driving the new car in the snow, and I didn't like it.

At that moment all I wanted to do was to drive to the car dealer and abandon the car like an unwanted pet. My daughter had a snow shovel in her car and, miraculously, freed my car from its icy clutches. It was a long driveway, packed with snow and deep ruts. I couldn't walk up the driveway to the house and there was no street parking. It was decided that I should give up the idea of staying at Susan's mother-in-law's house and go to my daughter and son-in-law's house which was not too far away and the drifts in their driveway had been plowed. That was a false start to my new life, but I had a second chance to begin my journey again.

Two days later, and I have no memory of those days either, I went to the closing of the house, which went smoothly and I immediately left for Philadelphia, where I had decided to return to live.

After all, Frank had told me, "Go home again."

The closing on my house went without a hitch. The buyer didn't attend, but wired his money instead. After the week that had just transpired, I felt too exhausted to drive to Philadelphia by myself and

I tried to hire someone to drive me. Logistics were problematic and so I ended up with two drivers. One man drove me from the Hamptons, where the closing was, into New York City and I arranged for another driver to drive me on the second leg of the trip to Philadelphia. He took the train from Philadelphia and met us at the Jitney (the Hampton's version of a bus) stop. Driver # 1 jumped out of the car and onto the Jitney for his return trip home to the Hamptons, and made the next bus with five minutes to spare. As he slid out from behind the steering wheel of my car, Driver # 2 replaced him in a nanosecond and we were on our way. Pretty slick, if I must say so. Anyone watching, might think it was some kind of criminal maneuver with that seamless driver switch or a slight of hand trick. First there was a short, stout man behind the steering wheel and in the blink of an eye, suddenly there was a very tall, very thin man sitting there.

The drive from New York City to Philadelphia is about three and a half hours on a good day. This was not a good day. Many of the roads still had piles of snow packed on the outside lanes which cut down the number of available driving lanes, and it was December 30th so people were already traveling for the upcoming New Year's weekend. The three and a half hours turned into five and a half hours. It was still very cold and the ground was covered with snow. I wore my heavy fur lined UGG boots. The longer I sat in the car, with my boots on and the heater turned all the way up, the more my very toasty feet swelled up. By the time I got to my friends' house in

Philadelphia I felt like I was wearing 10 pound blocks on my feet. UGG boots are supposed to be worn without socks as they are lined with sheepskin. I didn't think it was polite to take the boots off in the car and just sit there with bare feet and hadn't thought to bring socks. I thought that might be too gross although it was my car. I guess if I could have gotten out of the car and walked around occasionally, that would have helped my rapidly swelling feet, but sitting in one spot for almost five and a half hours did little to mitigate the problem.

LIVING IN MY CAR

Starting my new life in Philadelphia I was comforted by the fact that I had family and lots of close friends in the area. Most of the time, I knew how to get from one place to another without getting lost. It would be a fresh start, but one in which I already had a level of comfort. I decided that an apartment would suit me just fine, no more houses for me. I looked at many apartments, both in downtown Philadelphia and the near suburbs and I ended up choosing a co-op apartment in a building where I had previously lived before we moved to Water Mill. There was a certain level of familiarity as I already knew where the trash room and the recycle room were located. Many of the same building personnel still worked there, and I knew quite a few of the residents. My real estate agent cautioned me not to consummate the sale until after I had closed on my house, just to be on the safe side in case the deal fell apart at the last minute.

After I returned to Philadelphia, I spent the next two weeks moving from place to place--living at a friends' house in Philadelphia and visiting my son and daughter-in-law's home in Brooklyn. I had all my plastic bins, suitcases, etc. in my car. It was a wonder that there was anything left for the mover to put in the truck. I left some of my things at my friends' house and the rest in my car for the trip to Florida. In the two weeks that remained before leaving for Florida, I bought my new apartment and arranged for renovations to take place while I was staying in Florida for the next eight weeks. My driver,

"Dom," picked up my car and stuff the night before I was to fly to Florida. Although Dom had been recommended by some other friends, I had never met him. He had arranged to pick up my car about 7:00 p.m. at my friend's house. He rang the doorbell, introduced himself, I handed him the car keys, and off he went. I stood out outside in the dark and frosty night and watched Dom drive my car getting smaller and smaller as it went off down the street, only being able to follow it by the tail-lights, which were like a beacon in the dark. At the corner, I saw the brake lights go on and the left turn signal flickering as Dom turned left and then the car disappeared from sight. I had a brief moment of panic (something I was doing more and more) and wondered if I would ever see my car and stuff again. I had just given my car and all the things in my car to a perfect stranger. How did I know that this was the real Dom and not some sort of person masquerading as Dom? Silly me!

Two days later, friends picked me up at the West Palm Beach Airport and drove me to Ocean Pointe. When I arrived at the time share, despite my unfounded fears, Dom was already parked in front waiting for me. He unloaded my Florida gear into my little studio apartment and took off to go to the airport to fly back north. I would see him again in eight weeks for the return trip. I sat in my apartment alone, surrounded by my things. I wondered out loud, "Why am I here? I want to go home now." But the hard truth was that I had no home, nowhere else to go, but my car. I had sold my house and my new home was in shambles, not yet livable. And worst of all, Frank was not here so we could unpack and put everything away together like we had done the last nine years when we had arrived in Florida. We had the process down to a science and usually finished the job in less than an hour. We had figured out where everything went, like on a ship. We called the little round black wrought iron dining table (36" in diameter) the data center as it held, barely, both of our computers and the printer, and we ate our meals on the coffee table or out on the balcony. The plastic bin with the kitchen supplies was called the pantry closet, and the box with bathroom items like medicines, shampoos, etc. served as our linen closet. All this was an effort to make the little space more pleasant. But without Frank there, I couldn't figure out what do next. I was puzzled about what to do next as if I had never been here before. Overwhelmed to the point of almost being paralyzed in both my ability to think or physically act. I stared at the luggage, but dealing with it was out of the question. I would figure out what to do in the morning and somehow get out of there and go where?

I felt utterly alone and I had signed on for eight weeks. I did not think I could survive eight weeks, let alone tonight. I walked out onto my little balcony, I was on the seventh floor. The rail wasn't that high and there were two chairs and a table, easy enough to climb over the railing. I was sorely tempted to think about going over the railing. I stood out there for a long time, listening to the waves, and looking at the ocean and sky and trying not to look down. I thought about all the reasons why I shouldn't do that, but what stopped me (I guess I wasn't totally committed to such a terrible act) was that I was hungry. I guess low blood sugar made me think irrationally. I hadn't eaten since early that morning before I went to the airport and it was now after 4:00 p.m. What an excuse for not jumping off a balcony. I walked out of the apartment and down to the Tiki Bar (not my favorite place to eat, but there were no other restaurants in the immediate area) to get something to eat. As I rounded the corner of the pool, I heard several voices call out, "Deb, you're here."

Several people jumped up from their poolside chairs and rushed over to embrace me. "We are so sorry about Frank, but so happy that you came down this year." More than a few tears were spilled and a lot of hugs were shared. As I made my way down the path to the Tiki Bar, every few feet, more people came up to repeat the scene. Frank was a very popular person. He was one of those people who you could describe as being "bigger than life." He held court with several other men at a large round umbrella table near the pool. He chatted with everyone, told funny jokes, and did all kinds of word games like the New York Times crossword puzzle and Word Jumbles from the newspaper. One of the older gentlemen, who sat at the table with Frank saved his Word Jumbles all year from his hometown paper in Baltimore and brought them to Florida always knowing that Frank would come up with the right Jumble Words and quickly, and he would say to Frank each time he solved the puzzle, "Write it down. You are good!"

The people who were greeting me were friends and acquaintances, from all over the country and people we had met over the last nine years and, like us, came down every winter to the same place at the same time. Even though Frank and I were a team, they were my friends, too.

"Where are you going?"

"To get something to eat at the Tiki Bar."

"Bring it back here and sit with us at the table while you eat."

I got a hamburger and brought it back to eat by the pool. Soon I was surrounded by more people as they checked in or came down to sit by the pool area, and they, too came over to greet me.

"How about going out to dinner with us tomorrow night?"

Five minutes later someone else asked me to join them at dinner on Sunday night. And so it went over the next eight weeks. Some nights I had two or three invitations to go out to dinner or to join others for a little dinner party in their units. One night, I got a call from one of my friends,

"We grilled dinner on the barbeque and we have extra food. Can I bring dinner over to your unit?"

181

"Yes, what is this Meals on Wheels?"

I am sure that most of the group did not realize that their kind and caring intervention, and it was an intervention, made me feel included as an individual and not just as part of a couple. This may have saved my life that first day. The next morning I woke up and looked over my balcony at the sun and the view of the bright blue sky, the ocean, the Port of Palm Beach, and the Intercostal Waterway and proceeded to unpack my things and went off to the supermarket. I was still sad and missing Frank at every turn, but I was moving forward. When I went to the supermarket I cried (tears quietly sliding down my cheeks) at the delicatessen counter while waiting for my number to be called. Nobody noticed, or if they did, they didn't say anything, such as, "Are you alright?" Maybe they thought that the wait at the Deli counter was too long for me so I cried. We used to shop there as a team; one of us walked through the store picking up the other items on the shopping list and the other (usually Frank because I am not a very patient person in a waiting situation) waited in the deli line which was usually very long. I realized that now I only needed half as much sliced turkey and cheese and there was no point in buying Frank's favorite lunch items. Chalk up the super market experience to another first. I continue to struggle with this issue almost every time I go food shopping. Even today as I spot his favorite foods and place them in my basket, I forget for a moment that he is not home to eat them. Then I put them back.

Frank would have been 77 years old on February 7th, 2011. Since I was in Florida at that time I decided to have a celebration of his life (he had several such celebrations already) because the majority of his many friends at the resort had not been able to come to his funeral as most of them lived scattered around the northeast and Midwest. I made arrangements with the manager of the resort to use an outdoor covered pavilion which had a lot of tables and chairs and verbally invited everyone who was staying there who had considered themselves Frank and/or my friend to his birthday party.

"I am having a celebration of Frank's life on what would have been his 77th birthday on February 7th and I would like you to come."

The response that I got from almost every person was, "Great, we will be there. What can I bring?" I was planning on having pizzas delivered. I bought big bags of salad and dressing at Costco and told people;

"Bring beverages and dessert."

The day of the party, I was asked by several people,

"How many people are you expecting?"

"I don't know, somewhere between ten and forty" which I said half-jokingly because I had no idea. I didn't keep track of the number of

183

people I asked nor had I requested an RSVP. The management was so wonderful; they provided the set ups, plastic ware, plates, table cloths, etc. Although the weather was warm and sunny, the wind was howling all day and I was a little concerned. The event was called for 6:30 p.m., but at 6:00 p.m. the wind suddenly calmed down and it promised to be a beautiful tropical evening. Friends started to arrive, many carrying bottles of wine and desserts. Someone brought a big frosted sheet cake that said, "God Bless." Instead of sitting four to a table, the tables were pushed together to seat larger groups. All the guests knew each other, but some groups knew each other better. The common thread was Frank and I. Many friends sat down with people that they didn't know very well and before long everyone was chatting like best friends which Frank would have loved because he was all about friendships. I had ordered eleven pizzas delivered to the resort. I guess I could have used more as they ate all but one slice.

Various guests stood up and told anecdotes about Frank, some funny, some bittersweet. As I had hoped, everyone seemed to be in the spirit of celebrating his life. I did a head count and there were 56 guests present – so much for my estimate of 10-40 people. As I looked over the guests gathered at the tables, I noticed a middle age couple sitting by themselves hungrily eating their pizza and listening intently to the various speakers. I realized I had never seen them before. I walked over to a few friends and subtlety pointed the couple out and asked, "Do you know who those people are?" The answer from each person was, "No, I have never seen them before."

I never did find out who they were. I guess they were hungry and decided to join what they thought was a party. I don't know what they thought of the content of the speeches or if they ever realized the guest of honor was not even present. Perhaps they too were touched by the words offered by friends and the special ambience of the evening. The final number of people present was 54 friends and two strangers whom I never saw again. It was a wonderful evening filled with friendship and love, but I am not sure if I planned the event to celebrate Frank's life and his birthday, or if it was more for me, or both, and did it really matter? It certainly helped get me through what was a very tough day.

The time flew by in Florida. The eight weeks were over too quickly and it was time to go north, not home, because I still had no official home, other than my car. My apartment was five to six weeks from completion and I was in a quandary as to where I would live during that time that would suit my needs and not be too costly. The time in Florida spoiled me because I was always surrounded by a large number of caring friends and acquaintances. There was always someone around to talk to, eat with, and to go with me to the nearby movies or the mall. Now my situation was going to drastically change.

I decided that staying with family or friends up north for such a long time wouldn't work. I would be like the famous "man who came to dinner." What if my apartment took longer to complete than expected and I needed to stay longer? I felt that it would be an imposition and I wasn't too comfortable living in someone else's home for weeks. One of the most important criteria in finding a temporary place to live was the location and its proximity to my new apartment as I would have to be going over there almost daily to keep an eye on the final stage of the renovations. I checked out a lot of places and discovered that, over the years, I had amassed more than 400,000 Marriott points which would get me approximately five free weeks in a Marriott long-term stay hotel. Frank and I had planned to use those points for a vacation that we were going to take the summer that he got sick, but since that was no longer a consideration I would use them to pay for my temporary home--the third home (calling it a home might be stretching it a bit) in 10 weeks. I had located a Marriott Residence hotel about 20 minutes away from my new apartment that met all of my needs. Using my points - kind of like Monopoly dollars - I was able to get a small one bedroom suite with a kitchen. The door of the room had a brass colonial style door knocker in an attempt to make the hotel guest feel like they were home. Nice touch, but it didn't work for me. A friend drove me there and my driver met me at the hotel with my car and luggage and brought everything up to my room.

When they left, I looked around and realized just how alone I was. It was pretty tight quarters as the apartment was filled with my luggage, suitcases filled with winter and summer clothes, hanging clothes in the closet, one plastic tub with assorted paperwork and another with tax papers. The other plastic tubs, which contained kitchen supplies and other assorted items I left in my car until I moved into my apartment. There was a dresser in the apartment bedroom, but I was not capable of unpacking anything. I wanted to believe that I was just there for a few days and not for more than a month and so I lived out of my suitcases. The hotel served a continental breakfast, but I preferred to eat in my room at the tiny dining room table so I went down for my free newspapers, cup of tea, and a bagel and took it back up to my room.

Since it was a hotel designed for mostly business people, they also served a light dinner buffet from Monday to Thursday nights. I went down the first night and got even more depressed. The food didn't look comforting or appetizing, and it was served on paper plates with plastic silverware. It was akin to something that might be served at the high school cafeteria. Weary looking people, mostly men and often sitting alone, as they ate their dinner while reading, watching one of the flat screen TV's, or working on their computers. I filled a plastic bowl with some pretzels and cubes of cheese and another one with a small mixed salad and took it back to my room as my appetizer. Every night on my way back to the hotel from my apartment, I would stop at the supermarket and pick up some prepared dinner at a market and heat it up in the microwave.

One night I bought a small frozen pizza and was about to put it in the oven to heat, when I realized that there was no oven. There were only two stove-top burners and a microwave for cooking. I guess that is why it was called a kitchenette. And on my way to breakfast or dinner I stopped at the front desk of the hotel and talked to whichever clerk was on duty. The desk staff were the only people I got to know during my stay. They gave me cards and gifts for my birthday which touched me deeply. This was not like my stay in Florida where every time I opened my door there was someone around that I knew. I had my calendar book with me at all times, and every morning and night, and sometimes in-between I checked off the squares. I would count and recount the days remaining hoping that this might make the days go faster. It was like repeatedly pushing the elevator button in hope that it might arrive at your floor more quickly.

During the week, I would make the approximately 20 minute drive to my new apartment on a daily basis and see what was going on, and if there were any decisions to be made. Then I would go sit in the lobby of the apartment building as there was nowhere to sit in the apartment with all the building materials piled up and debris on the floor and workmen running around. The lobby became my temporary office as I sat there and made phone calls and did paperwork. I became a fixture in the lobby as old and new friends would stop and chat and often invite me to their apartments for lunch or a cup of tea. What I really wanted was to take a nap in the afternoon, but I didn't want to ask and no one offered me a spare bed.

Several times I went up to New York for the weekend to visit my family, and friends often came by to pick me up to go out to dinner. Of all the places I stayed during those four months, this was the worst. I did feel like I was living in my car, and in a way I was, the trunk and back seat were filled with my belongings that I didn't need right now or that I couldn't fit into my cramped room. Living in a hotel by oneself, might sound like fun to some folks, but I think it is a pretty lonely experience, especially when that is your only home. Other than having someone make your bed, clean the bathroom, give you fresh towels, and clean the kitchen every day, there is not much to be said to recommend the experience. I put it right up there on my own "most pathetic" list, just under the night after my tooth extraction. Fortunately I didn't have many items on my "poor me" list.

MOVING DAY—II

My move into my new home in Philadelphia was finally approaching. Besides the physical act of moving into my new apartment it loomed as a very emotional moment. I had never moved into any home without Frank being beside me. He didn't much care for moving as he didn't like change so I took charge of the process. I knew that the next day he would be fine with it all and would always tell me how much he appreciated my handling the move. My contractor, who was both a friend and my resident fairy godfather, worked on a very tight schedule so he could finish the renovation and I could move into my new home as quickly as possible. He only missed the promised date by five days. By then I had run out of Marriott hotel points and patience. The last few days of my stay in the hotel, I started to move my belongings over to my apartment and put them on the floor, covered by drop cloths, in an area where the work had been completed. Perhaps I did move in a little prematurely, but it was a wonderful feeling to be "home" again. For the first week, before the movers came with my belongings, it was a lot like camping out, but I didn't mind. I had a beautiful new kitchen without any pots, pans, or dishes. It is amazing what you can cook with an electric frying pan and a microwave. I had two bathrooms without any shower curtains or glass shower doors. The first time I showered, all the water came out on to the floor until I learned how to direct my new shower spray properly. I had ordered a set of twin beds for my guest room which is where I would sleep until the movers brought my bed. The mattress company didn't quite get the "s" at the end of "beds." I had ordered twin beds, but they only delivered one. However, since I only needed one bed to sleep in, I could wait for the other since I wasn't expecting company.

I had packed a set of sheets, from my old house to bring with me in case I needed them when I came back from Florida. They were queen size sheets and the bed was a single and I looked a lot like a mummy wrapped up in the queen size sheets and blanket as it was not possible to tuck them in. I bought another TV table to use as a night table, and during the day I moved it into the dining room for meals. I had packed my base unit phone and one hand held set, but it didn't do me any good because the phone company seemed to have repeated trouble coming out on the date promised, so I just relied on my cell phone. My neighbor, who I didn't previously know, knocked on my door and offered me any number of things to temporarily furnish my apartment. She lent me a card table and four chairs which became my new dining room set and a floor lamp. I purchased a rectangular folding table at the office supply store for use as my computer desk. I was pretty much set for the interim. Only one week to go until the movers came with my furniture and other assorted belongings, and the rest of my clothes. Every morning I had to be up, showered, and dressed before 8:00 a.m. as that is when the all the contractors came. There was still a lot to be done, but I had every faith that they would finish in time.

The week flew by and it was finally moving day. It was the end of April so there was no blizzard to worry about. The movers, although they were coming from Long Island City, New York, were at my apartment by 9:00 a.m. It was organized chaos on this end of the move, but more peaceful and less emotional than the moving out process. It was the beginning of my tomorrows and not an ending. It was a team approach to moving--there were four movers, two organizers, two designers, two contractors and me, and it is only a two bedroom apartment. A friend left his Chevy Suburban in the parking lot behind the apartment building so that things that didn't fit or I decided I didn't want to use, could be loaded right into it to be taken to a nearby consignment shop. By 6:00 p.m., the movers were nearly done. They called me into my bedroom to show me what they had accomplished. Unbeknownst to me, they had unpacked all the hanging clothes into my closet and taken the cardboard wardrobes away. It was a little overwhelming because all the clothes were shoved together without any master plan. I had no complaints. I appreciated what they had done. The organizers said, "Don't worry we will take care of it." Within a few hours they had all the clothing so neat and organized, even by color that it looked like a replica of one of the old Benetton sweater stores. I have always been very cautious of moving any items for fear I will mess up their design scheme, and maybe they will come back and check on me and I will not get a passing grade. The ultimate surprise was that when I turned around, I saw that several movers had made my bed. I had an ivory colored iron frame on my bed and they had put it together and there were two big cartons filled with bedding, sheets, pillow cases, pillows, blankets, a quilt, etc. Two of the movers were smiling broadly as they stood back from the bed admiring their work. They had put the dust ruffle on, and all of the bedding together as if they do this every day for customers. This sight was a first for me, as I never knew a movers' jobs was to make up your bed. It was fine with me. I will admit that the quilt was on in the wrong direction and the decorative pillows, I have a lot of them, were all jumbled on the bed in no apparent order. I smiled and thanked them for their turn down service. The only thing missing was the chocolate mint on my pillow. As they gathered their moving tools and prepared to leave, Avi, the boss, looked at me and smiled and said, "See? No tears today." I guess he remembered the night we moved out of my house in the Hamptons with the tears sliding down my cheeks.

When everyone finally left that night, I could hardly wait to get into my bed which I had not slept in for four long months. I did not mind that the bedding was not on correctly, nor did I even think of remaking it. I slept very well because I was home again, albeit a different home, in my own bed, and surrounded by many of my personal treasures that gave me a great level of comfort even if my husband could not be with me. I woke up a few times during the night and I smiled as I looked around my bedroom and recognized some cherished things, familiar items. In a few weeks all the pictures would be hung and my favorite personal items would be sitting on shelves and table tops just like in my other home. A few weeks later, a letter appeared in the mail, about the size and shape of a greeting card, with a hand written envelope and the mover's return address in the upper left hand corner. I thought maybe he was sending me an additional bill or some other business communication. Was I so surprised when I opened the envelope to find a note hand written on the mover's personal stationary thanking me for the opportunity to move me into my new home and it was signed by the owner of the company. No wonder he is such a successful mover. I guess his mother taught him manners.

WHO AM I? WHO WILL I BE NEXT?

The first time I went to a new doctor after Frank's death, I was asked to fill out a lengthy health history form. There is nothing unusual about that. Little blocks to mark with either a checkmark or an "x" offered me a variety of marital choices such as "Married," "Single," "Divorced," "Separated" or "Widowed." Since I had recently returned to the area, I would have to repeat this scenario in the next few months as I connected to new doctors. I was stymied by these questions.

I had never really looked at these categories before. I always dutifully checked off "Married." I think I was always married and if there was a life before marriage, my mother must have filled out the form for me. I wondered, "What difference did it make what my marital status was in relation to my medical treatment?" I felt that these choices were somewhat judgmental and I couldn't decide if I should check "Single" or "Widowed" as they were both correct.

The first time I went to a new doctor, I checked "Single." After that, when visiting a new doctor, I usually varied my answers between "Single" and "Widowed" as an experiment for the medical professional to see if that led to any questions or concerns that they cull from this information. Maybe the medical professional reading my chart would ask in response to a check for widow, "Are you sad?" or for a divorced person, "Do you have custody of your children?" I never remember any medical person treating me any differently based on my answer or asking me even one question pertaining to my marital status. Probably they never even looked at the little box or even cared what my marital state was. I have been tempted to check off "Divorced" or "Separated" and see where that leads me. Recently I was at a doctor's office and was given a form to fill out and I noticed a new approach. "Single/widowed/divorced" was all lumped together as one category space and the doctor was not asking for any differentiation of the single marital status. I preferred being lumped in with the whole unmarried group. It lent an air of mystery to my status.

WIDOW'S WEEDS

I liked my old life. I think that I didn't know what real love was until I didn't have it anymore. I didn't know that it would end so soon and I didn't treasure our time together enough. At least that is the way I look at it now. I see other couples and want to tell them, "Hold on to each other tightly, speak nicely to each other, tell your partner at least twice a day that you love them or it might be too late, even sooner than you think." I was married for almost 54 years. A marriage, particularly a long one, ebbs and flows over the years, sometimes it was good, and sometimes not so good. The last ten years of our marriage were the best of them all. I think that the whole perspective changes when your spouse dies. You can only look backwards at your marriage and there is no future to it. The door has closed on it except for memories.

During our marriage, we had taken a number of vacations to the Mediterranean, including to Greece and Italy. During these trips I observed the widows' customs. Some widows in this country, who are of Mediterranean origin also follow the same path. These same customs may apply in other cultures, but I am unaware of them. These customs relate to how women dress after the death of their husbands. After I became a widow, I remembered what I had noticed on my travels and it made a lot of sense to me. As soon as their husbands die, and they do seem to expect that their husbands may indeed die before them, they put that part of their life behind them.

197

They put on their black dresses and cover their heads with black scarves and shawls immediately after their husbands pass away. The widow's uniform must be waiting in the back of the closet or folded in tissue paper and cradled in a bed of moth balls in a chest of drawers, perhaps even passed down from generation to generation to be readily available. This outfit is worn as a badge of sorts to denote that they are now widowed and have moved on to the next stage of life. Their garb acknowledges that something has happened, something is wrong. When you look at the Mediterranean widows, you immediately know a lot about them without anyone having to ask questions, like, "How is your husband." or "How are you doing?" They can talk widowspeak to each other because they can easily identify who the other widows are.

These widows seem to be better prepared, as opposed to me, because they know what to do, at least Step 1, by putting on the widow's weeds. They don't have Match.com or Jdate and the widows don't seem to want to go in that direction either. I think that it would be helpful if, we had widow's weeds, too. I think that we used to have them in the earlier times in this country, but the wearing of black for a year, or even for life, after the death of one's husband has gone out of vogue in most of the United States. In the Jewish religion, anyone whose loved one has died, usually wears a small black button attached to a cut black ribbon for thirty days or throughout the first year after the funeral, but I noticed that often when people see it and recognize it, they look away. If I see the black ribbon, I usually offer my condolences to the person, "I am sorry for your loss." I think that we need a more updated version of widow's weeds.

NEW FRIENDS

A friend and former neighbor recommended that I join a national group that had local chapters in many cities, for women over 50 whose lives are in transition. It includes widows, divorcees, recently moved, recently retired or those having a partner that recently retired, empty nest syndrome, etc. This encompasses just about every woman in the over 50 age range. I think my friend didn't quite know what to do with me so she pointed me to The Transition Network (TTN), and in hindsight it turned out to be a positive suggestion. I certainly qualified for membership as a person whose life was in transition. They hold local monthly peer meetings in the private homes of members who live in the neighborhood and also have city wide events that include women from the other chapters in the Philadelphia area. I had a panic attack just driving one mile to the first meeting, my version of kicking and screaming. It felt like I was going to my first day of kindergarten and my mother wouldn't take me or watch me lovingly from the door to make sure I was all right. I didn't want to go, but I thought it would be "good for me." It seems in the early days after Frank's death, that I made a lot of decisions based on whether I thought it would be good for me or someone else thought it would be good for me. Maybe that is good philosophy as any to use as a base for decisions.

I didn't like any of these new people or the activities they offered. I hated it all. At the first meeting, new members were given five minutes to introduce themselves (it is called "checking in") and to say what brought them to the group. I said I had been widowed within the year and had sold my home and moved four times in the last four months. I thought that was enough transitions to qualify. I decided not to mention the murder of my daughter more than thirty years ago. There wasn't enough time, in the five minutes allotted to me, for all my major life transitions and I thought that I had shared enough for the first time. I didn't want to shock them or make them feel sorry for me. This peer group was definitely not where I wanted to be that evening even though at the end of the meeting, several of the women came up to me and acknowledged how difficult life must be for me with all those transitions. They each handed me a piece of paper which had their name and phone number on it and told me I could call them anytime I wanted to meet for lunch or to take a walk. They were reaching out to me and I was touched by the gesture, but I wasn't ready to move to the next level of friendships with these seemingly nice, but new acquaintances. I am usually pretty garrulous, but except for my five minute introductory speech, I was pretty quiet. If I had reinvented myself, I may have picked the wrong person.

As soon as the meeting was over, I skipped the refreshments and bolted out the door for home. It all felt strange and foreign to me, as if I had been dropped from the planet Krypton, without a magic cape, into a totally new life. And, that is exactly what it was. I did join the group and I decided that, in a year, after my membership expired, I would not renew it. It wasn't for me. I pushed myself to go to the meetings and some of the events, but I continued to be resistant. Then one day after about nine months, I realized I was looking forward to going to the peer group that night and seeing the women and listening to the enlightening discussions that we would have. I even stayed after the meeting to socialize with other members. I started to car pool with some of my new friends (I had moved from the acquaintance level to the friend level) to go to many of the interesting events and places I might not have gone by myself. This was a new paradigm for me, getting out in the world with the goal of making new girlfriends. It took time and focus, but it was worth the effort as a new life opened up in front of me, one that I had never considered before.

I have belonged to TTN for almost 7 years now. It is an integral and important part of my life. As I was told from the beginning, the peer group is not meant to be a support group. The woman who introduced me to TTN was most emphatic about that which I didn't quite understand at first. It can be viewed as a transition from a bereavement group and stands on its own merits. There are monthly meetings with a different focus each month. It's not unusual for us to spontaneously veer off topic because a member may have a special need to discuss a different item. The meeting is still worthwhile whatever the topic. The women had become my sisters and empowered me to transition to whatever I was called upon to handle in life. In one's lifetime, we operate within many different circles of friends. While married, I felt that my primary circle consisted of my husband and other couples, married or otherwise. After being widowed, the circles widen and contract, some more important than others. I found that TTN had become very important to me as it introduced me to additional friends that I would not have met otherwise. These widening circles provided me with a doorway to new activities and new people. If my husband had not passed away, these experiences would not have existed. If my husband were still alive, he would still be my primary social circle.

I was expanding my horizons and having fun doing it and I was in charge of the process. I have a reputation for having a good sense of humor. I was invited to prepare a brief, but humorous speech for my TTN friends. About 95 women were expected to attend the speech. The topic was to present the results of a questionnaire and to do it in an entertaining manner and in eleven and a half minutes. The questionnaire included 19 topics. I have given speeches before, but not amusing ones (that I know of). I did not prepare the speech ahead of time, but only read over the questions and answers to familiarize myself with the subject matter. The speech was more than funny and I had a good time presenting it. I made it with a half minute to spare. My friends thought I was very funny and several people suggested I become a standup comic. I assume that they were kidding, but I took it as a compliment. I don't think I could ever have duplicated that speech; it was a once in a lifetime accomplishment.

Most of my friends and social activities revolved around my husband and me as a couple. I had been in this situation for more than fifty years and I began to realize that was a long time. I had originally thought that when I moved back to the Philadelphia area I would just pick up again with many of my old friends, but surprisingly, that isn't the way it happened. Some of my friends were still very much there for me, but some of my old friends in Philadelphia seemed happy to see me again, but I was no longer part of their lives and they had moved on. A few made lunch dates with me, while I really would have preferred to go out to dinner because the time between cooking and eating my dinner at home and bedtime was very long. I didn't get many dinner invitations as many of my friends had husbands or partners although some took a night off from their busy lives to invite me to join them for dinner. I have observed that widows seem to get lunch, not dinner invites. It was necessary for me to find a new cadre of friends unless I wanted to stay home by myself and I didn't relish going places alone, especially if I had to drive at night. Looking back, I guess I was making progress although at the time, I didn't see it. At first, I told a little fib and said that I couldn't see very well at night (true sometimes, depending on where I was going) and got people to pick me up to go to the group's meetings or events. If I were going in town to meet friends for dinner, I would take a train or bus and then, if it were dark, a cab or Uber home. I was finding that the thought of driving more than ten minutes alone at night pretty scary. Then one day, I just got in my car and drove in town and parked my car in my favorite parking lo without giving it much thought.

Shortly after I moved into my apartment I heard that there was to be a bingo game in our community room. I thought maybe I could handle that. Wrong! I would head to the door of my apartment but I couldn't open it. I was pacing around the apartment. After a number of false starts I finally propelled myself out the door and down to the community room. There about six people there and I didn't know any of them. The experience was a tad daunting but I enjoyed myself, I made 5 new acquaintances, and I won $3.00 in my foray into the social world. That was my first and last Bingo game in the apartment building because they never offered it again. I wish they had scheduled another bingo game, I was ready to go again and win some more money. There are times when I was invited to join some of my new friends to go out but I would have preferred to stay home alone. Most of the time I get myself off the sofa, put some lipstick on, take a deep breath, and out I go with the girls and I am glad I did. I met such interesting new women who had led fascinating lives. We are less distracted in our lives after fifty and can focus more on building new friendships.

It isn't that people were not willing to establish new relationships, not like in high school where girls had cliques and could be catty and mean. Friendships with women over fifty were very different than with younger women. Children are no longer a factor anymore in this process. When our children were in school, women often struck up friendships with the parents of their children's friends because they had children as the common denominator. For women who worked, friendships were often formed in the workplace. On-line dating services are not much help in finding new female friends, although there are some social networks that may be available for this task. It is lot of work to find and make new friends. I needed to develop some new skills and that doesn't happen overnight. Sometimes it feels that it would be easier to become an agoraphobic and just sit home watching TV, reading, and working on the computer. There is some similarity between meeting new female friends and meeting men. I think that the main difference has to do with the emotional tone of the relationship. If you meet a woman and find that your interests and goals are not compatible, following through in establishing or not establishing a friendship is not laden with the same kind of angst than it would be with a man.

Friendships with women can have a group dynamic and, not always involve a one-on-one relationship. Fear of rejection is not usually an area of great concern when meeting new women. Auditioning for a friendship with women is very different than trying out for a date with a man. The concept of competition doesn't come into play. As we have learned from research done over the years, nurturing relationships with other women is good for our health. Women develop friendships with other women in a far different way and for different reasons than men form relationships with other men.

Women offer support systems and share feelings that they utilize in helping each other deal with life and its ups and downs. Friendships with other women can be a very important and necessary component in one's life and there is no limit on age when it comes to making new women friends. I found this out when Frank died. He truly had been my best friend, and I never felt the need to expand my circle. Until that moment, I felt I had enough friendships with other women, most of them spouses of couples in our social circle or family members that were contemporaries. I had no reason to seek out new friends at this time of my life. I thought I was too old to make new friends. While Frank was alive, if I wanted to do something, I usually did it with Frank. Once I better understood that the responsibility to make new friends was mine and that I had the capacity to open myself to the possibilities of different kinds of relationships it got easier. The alternative was to find myself alone. Who likes to be alone all the time? I decided that was not for me.

Almost three years later, I had found so many new "girlfriends" and I have places to go and friends that are available to go with me in ever widening circles. I didn't believe it at first, but what I had been told was true, it is the women who pull you through, at least in the beginning. Most of the time, I also have a choice--to be alone or not to be alone. I am living a life that I did not ever envision for myself. Is it better than my other life that I lived with my husband? No way. The best that can be said about it is that it is based on a different model: the new normal. And I learned that working through this new paradigm does not happen overnight. I am too impatient, but working on it. I have also begun to be content with my own company. I learned that I don't always have to be with other people.

Over time, I came to some important insights. Some were what can be called an "aha" moment which arrives in a sudden burst of clarity; others came to me, albeit more slowly. I began to accept that my life had changed and would continue to change; there was no endpoint or goal. There was no going back. Changes are not easy to integrate into one's life whether they are changes that we plan for or desire or not, and they are all stressful. I can't say that the loss of my husband is worse than the next widow's loss; it is just different and it is mine alone. In dealing with grief and loss, there is an accepted arc that has been presented to us over the years by various experts in the field. This includes stages or steps that we have to go through to help us on our journey. Rather than just dealing with the accepted stages of grief and loss, although they must be addressed in the process, I think there are at least three additional phases in the cycle of change. We often have to go through them simultaneously while experiencing grief and loss. It is difficult to control as much of this process occurs in a spontaneous manner. These phases can also be considered in a circular manner, two steps forward, one step back and so on.

The initial stage, the death of one's partner when you enter the state of widowhood, is a fait accompli and no matter how hard you try, it cannot be altered, although I certainly tried. You can get stuck there for a while, I know I did. Sometimes you need help climbing out or you think you are done, and then you slip back. I discovered that this is part of normalizing your life. The next step is "now," being in the moment. No matter what the issue is being here now is almost always very difficult to achieve. I call this the state of indecision. I think that this may be the most disconcerting and anxiety provoking time and it can go on for a very long time. It is a period of transition and confusion. Decisions may need to be made and I wondered, "Is this the right thing to do? Should I do it now or wait until later?" This is where "They" come into the picture again. It is part of the unwritten handbook of admonishments; "Don't make any important decisions for a year." If you can follow that rule, it may decrease the chance of making mistakes. Of course, then it paralyzes your thought processes and leaves you in a quandary as to what to do next--do this or do that. This second part of this equation can be so difficult, because there is often a strong pull to go back to the past – your comfort zone. At this juncture it is where you can begin building the new normal. When Frank was alive we often went out on Saturday night to dinner or the movies, sometimes by ourselves and sometimes with other couples. Now it fell on me to do these activities by myself or with girlfriends or to simply stay home. I was faced with constructing a whole new paradigm. It was necessary to think outside the box or you might get stuck in it. During the first year after Frank passed away, it was not an easy task to make plans, but as the first year passed, I got tired of sitting home alone every weekend and I began to slowly move on. I guess you could call it baby steps. I had to look back over the months to see that I was surprised that I had been making progress, even taking into consideration the occasional act of regressing. It took a few years, but now I have many new friends and I find that on weekends, I have a lot of wonderful activities to choose from and friends to spend time with. I usually start planning my weekend activities by mid-week and so I have things to look forward to every week. The third step, achieving the new normal, is more elusive and difficult to maintain. The goal of getting over it is much too simplistic, because it doesn't happen, but you can have a happy and productive life again, albeit a different one.

THE ELEPHANT IN THE ROOM

For almost 54 years of my married life, I thought I owned the plural pronoun "we." That also extended to words like "our" and "us." Those words are a part of me and I can't completely erase them from my vocabulary like some kind of word-specific aphasia. In the early months after Frank's passing, and occasionally to this day, I still find myself using the "we" words in conversation with others. Sometimes the "we" surprises me as it subconsciously escapes my lips. When the "we" words leave my lips, certain people, not those who are closest to me, audibly inhale and avert their eyes and try to pretend that they didn't hear it by changing the subject. I usually use the word in talking about something in the past, when I was a "we" and to refer to that time or experience as an "I" would feel artificial and uncomfortable. To verbally erase the term and correct, although I have at times, it draws even more attention to it. It leads to bigger and more elephants in the room. There were times when I gave up any attempts at conversation except dealing with the weather or simple requests like "Please pass the salad." Initially, I made a conscious effort to avoid the company of people that I did not know well. Otherwise in most social settings, I remained mute, perhaps responding to the conversation that I wasn't paying much attention to with a simple nod of the head or a tentative smile.

In the first year or so after Frank's death, when I met people I knew in a public place like a restaurant, or entered a room of people that I not seen since his death, I usually got one of two responses: 1) people would offer their condolences accented by a hug or a light touch on your arm and move on. This is what I prefer. Saying something, I feel is better than not saying anything. 2) Some people avert looking at you directly and say nothing that would give you a clue as to whether they know or not. If they don't make eye contact, it is usually a tip-off that they do know that Frank passed away, but they don't want to or can't articulate it. More likely they do know and have created an elephant in the room, i.e., Frank, who actually becomes more visible, and I, the widow, felt more invisible. One day, in the food market, I saw a man who used to do business with Frank. He recognized me and said "hello," and then stood there mutely. I finally said, "Do you know that Frank passed away?" as that was our connection.

"Yes, I was at the funeral."

At that point we were both fumbling for words and there was really no need to talk further.

"Nice seeing you," I said.

"Nice to see you, too."

Some people think I am contagious and for that reason, they don't want to talk about "it." They put me in the cone of silence because

212

they are afraid if they articulate what happened it will rub off on them. Many family members and friends welcome the elephant in the room. Some close friends and I have a game we play in a restaurant when we are looking over the menu. We put together a meal that Frank might have ordered if he were with us. He enjoyed eating and ate his many favorite foods with enthusiasm. He was not always as compliant as he could have been with his low fat diet and the caloric content of his meal. In his fantasy meal, we order all the things he might have chosen, regardless of the fat and calorie content and that includes blueberry pie and, of course, with vanilla ice cream on top. In the end, it didn't much matter what he had eaten any way. My therapist says that Frank doesn't always have to be there, but it isn't possible to avoid it. It is not just me who brings him into the room; other people bring him into the empty chair as well. In some ways it is more difficult for me, but on the other hand, I really appreciate that I am not the only one who misses him. He still is with us all.

TABLE FOR ONE--PART II

One summer Sunday, less than a year into my widowhood, I took myself out to a late breakfast at a popular neighborhood delicatessen. Going out to Sunday breakfast was a weekly ritual from my other life that I hadn't thought about reestablishing until now. In the Hamptons we always went out to the same Greek restaurant, The Candy Kitchen, and ordered the same thing every week, no need for menus. Everyone that worked there knew us and made the eggs the way we liked them without us even having to say how we wanted them prepared. We used to sit in a booth near the counter and read our Sunday newspaper as we ate our breakfast. I really missed our Sunday breakfast so I thought now that I was back in the Philadelphia area, I would try it again on my own. I had eaten at that delicatessen many times before I had moved away to the Hampton's.

A line of customers were waiting for a table. I was feeling a little uncomfortable already among the sea of people I did not know. I got into the line and the hostess asked, "How many are in your party?"

"One, please," I responded.

She picked up a menu and said, "Follow me, I can seat you now."

I should have wondered why she plucked me out of line with so many hungry people waiting in line ahead of me. When I was escorted to my table, I began to understand why I was singled out, both literally and figuratively, for this special table for one. It may be the strangest table in any restaurant in North America. It is located right in the middle of the restaurant and it has a waist high wall around three sides. It strongly resembles a witness box in a courtroom. There were two chairs, but due to the lack of space in this cubicle, one chair was pushed up so tightly against the table that no one could sit there. I couldn't even put my purse on it; it was a true table for one. I wasn't too comfortable sitting there alone. I felt that I had a sign over my head that said, "NEWLY BEREAVED WIDOW." I felt obvious and invisible at the same time. For some other people, widowed or not, it might not be an issue, but I was feeling rather bereft as I tried to eat my meal in the middle of this large restaurant alone. I was completely surrounded by couples or families who were eating and enjoying themselves.

About two months later I found myself at the same restaurant at lunch time. I decided to try again. There were two hostesses this time and I was immediately offered the table for one which I strongly declined. I felt like I was being put in the time-out chair for unacceptable behavior, like being widowed. If I wanted to eat at a table for one, I could stay home. The hostess said, "Well then you are going to have to wait for a table."

I noticed there were plenty of tables for two, so I'm not sure what she had in mind for me. The hostess proceeded to seat couples that were behind me in line at the tables for two; I was the only single in line. I probably should have walked out, but instead I approached the other hostess and told her what had transpired.

"I won't sit there. I feel it is very insulting and if you can't find me another table now, I am going to leave and never come back again," I told her.

I guess I sounded like a petulant child. The hostess didn't seem too moved by my threat to leave as the restaurant was so busy that the loss of one customer, me, wouldn't greatly impact their level of business.

"The other person is new and doesn't know what she is doing. I will get you a better table," the hostess said.

She showed me to a large booth that seated eight. Now I had gone from the ridiculous to the sublime. It is like they say, "Be careful what you wish for, you might get it." If I thought that I stuck out like a sore thumb at the table for one, a single person sitting in a booth for eight during the busy lunch hour looks odd as well. I wondered why the hostess put me at such a big booth; was she being unkind? I looked even more alone as if the rest of my party did not show up. It would be helpful if informal restaurants like delicatessens would offer seating at a counter where people who are alone can sit and enjoy their meal. At a counter you have some choices; you can often strike up an interesting conversation with someone sitting next to you or even with the chef or cooks or choose not to interact with others. I usually put my Kindle in my purse when I know I am going out to eat alone, so I can read rather than just looking around or staring down at my food. A communal table is also an option. I have noticed that some nicer restaurants have started to offer what are called, "high-top tables" in the bar area where a single person can sit alone, but still be surrounded by other diners.

I have never gone back to that restaurant alone. I will only go with a group of people when it is their choice. I always glance over at the table for one to see if anyone is seated there and if they have any reaction to it. Most of the time the table sits empty and forlorn, just like many of the people whom they attempt to seat there.

Approximately a year later, I was watching the local early morning news show on TV and saw that at about 5:30 a.m., a large red pick-up truck crashed through the front window of the delicatessen and plowed deep into the restaurant. The restaurant was not yet open so there were no customers. Some kitchen workers were on the other side of the restaurant, but none were injured. Other than the original news report, there was never any additional information on the accident except that the repairs would be completed in time for the delicatessen to reopen the next morning for breakfast. I did not have a reason to go there for a few months. When I returned to eat with some friends I told my story of the table for one. As I looked around

217

the room, I realized that the table for one was gone. I couldn't believe it. The truck accident had obliterated it and the area was rebuilt so all the tables were the same size, tables for two. I am not sure why the table had disappeared; maybe other customers had complained about that little sad table or the contractor who was making the repairs had asked, "What is that?" I was not sorry to see it go, one more thing that I didn't have to think about anymore. It doesn't matter now. When I do go there these days I am usually with a group of friends and we have to ask the host for a large table.

I talked to my neighbor who has been widowed for a long time, about the issue of eating alone in a public place. Her response was, "I would rather stay home and eat sawdust than go to a restaurant alone." Another friend who is widowed doesn't mind going to restaurants alone especially to more upscale ones. She suggests that this is a good approach as they always treat her nicely and give her a lovely table. I bet the hostess doesn't seat her at a terrible table for one. She thinks this is preferable to always staying home and eating alone. But she is not your average grieving widow. Her face and name are recognizable to many, so maybe that helps. She may eat alone, but she isn't alone, with people coming over to her table, to greet her. So there you have it. There are choices and you have to pick and choose for what feels right for you and when. And your decisions may change from time to time and from year to year, but I will try to stay away from any table for one.

MUSINGS ON THE GRIEF OF WIDOWHOOD

As I approached the first year anniversary after Frank's death, there were days when I didn't know what to do with my pain. It hurt so much that I could hardly breathe. Every day it got worse and there didn't seem to be an end in sight. I had some thoughts about killing myself to get rid of the pain, a condition often referred to as "suicidal ideation." These were thoughts and not actions. When Frank was so sick, I asked him if he wanted me to go with him, hand in hand, but he was adamant that I not do that. Maybe that is the coward's way. I tried focusing on what a horror that would be for my children and grandchildren. If I didn't keep that in mind, maybe I would have more seriously considered it.

Dealing with these thoughts is a very exhausting process with the emotional tugging one way and then the other. I was not just trying to get rid of the pain. I wanted to be reunited with my honey, but there was some trepidation in that as well. I was fearful that maybe he wouldn't be there waiting for me and then I will be sitting there alone until infinity. I am probably going to go through the rest of my life alone without a partner, but I do have my family and friends. Reading these thoughts may be shocking to some. I find it hard to believe that others have not thought these dark thoughts as well, particularly in the first year, or possibly longer. These ideations do serve as a bridge to cross from the past to the present until they slowly recede. Being Jewish, I was taught to believe that there is no life after death. I have since come to learn that Jews do believe in "the world to come." I don't think I buy that, nor do I want to buy that. I think that having some level of suicidal ideation is not unusual after the death of a loved one, although most people don't talk about it. It's only serious if the thoughts are relentless and then it is time to see a professional. This is where one's resilience is tested.

Many widows tell me that the pain is always there, but as time goes by (no, time does not heal) it becomes less harsh and the edges less sharp. You learn to hide it better, even from yourself. The jury is still out for me on that. I sometimes still feel lonely and empty, but that is my secret. My life is quite busy and that does keep me out and about. Busy is a good thing—it fills the days and hours and brings a sense of normalcy to my life. I serve on the board of directors for the Anti-Violence Partnership of Philadelphia (AVP). The board has lots of meetings that fill up my days and evenings. I founded the AVP in 1980, two years after our daughter, Nancy, was murdered. AVP provides services for people who have had a family member murdered. One of the reasons that I moved back to Philadelphia was to return to my work with AVP. It was something that I felt passionate about and know that I can make a difference in other people's lives. I enjoyed being involved in these activities and it makes me feel more at peace with the world. People who know me say, "I am so proud of you. You are so strong." Of course, that is the way they wanted me to be and I didn't want to disappoint them.

After barely eating regular meals for a year, one of my big daily activities became planning my dinner. I noticed that I ate more dinners out with friends on the weekends and occasionally during the week, but generally speaking I ate most dinner's at home. I don't really mind. I have gotten used to my table for one. I have made some rules for eating alone. I am a good cook, although I don't like just cooking for myself. I accompany my dinner with a small glass of red wine (doctor's orders). I was a little concerned about having a drink alone, I only drink wine, and never more than one glass at a sitting so that seems OK. I never eat my dinner earlier than 6:30 p.m. to keep the evening from being too long before bedtime. I watch TV while I eat at my kitchen counter and sometimes I also read. I have turned mealtimes into a multi-tasking event which is a habit that I started within a few weeks of Frank's death. After dinner sometimes I still feel hungry, but that is an emotional hunger and I think that I am just feeling empty. A good meal and a nice glass of wine do not fill the hole in my heart.

As a professional social worker specializing in working with issues of grief and bereavement, I now realize that much of what I discussed with clients was often less than what they were looking for. There are many types of therapies. The therapist or counselor does not have to have gone through a similar experience to be able to provide helpful counseling. The loss of a partner is one of those presenting issues that I feel therapists may be more helpful if they, too, have experienced the same loss. This does not mean to say that the support offered is not sufficient if the therapist does not share the same event. It is just different. It is not necessary, probably not even recommended that the counselor divulge the fact that they have a shared experience with the client. Any interaction between client and counselor should never be about the therapist, but focus on the client. In this case, the fact that the counselor personally shares the experience, gives a very different perspective. I don't feel that things that I have told clients were harmful to them, but I may have missed the point and let them down.

For example, one of my mantras which I've told newly bereaved people was, "One cannot travel under, over, or around the pain, grief, and sadness, but you must go through it." That is easier said than done. When I tried that on for size, I realized that this might be a futile quest. I wondered to myself, "Will I ever come out the other side?" I think I am very afraid that I might get stuck part way, like crawling through a pipe. The statement is true, you need to go through it, there is no alternative, but it is only a goal. Maybe a widow could hire a surrogate or professional widow to go through it for them, this way it gets done without all the attendant pain, but if only it was that easy.

I know that no one warned me about the travails of this journey. It is very difficult to achieve and takes a lot of time and energy. Sometimes I think it is likened more to traversing a maze than going straight through a passageway to the end because there is no end.

Now I know what Freud was talking about when he said, "Grief is work." I better understood that what I was explaining to bereaved people was only half true, and I didn't take into account the difficulties involved. I didn't fully understand the ramifications of that statement which was meant to instruct the griever on how to get through the journey. Eventually most grievers will get through it, but each in their own time and in their own way. As time goes on, the dichotomy of the two grievers, one being the part that gets internalized, and is always there, and the other part the public persona. As time passes, that façade becomes easier to display to the world. And that makes people believe that you are doing much better than you really are. I often hear, "You are looking so much better than last year." If they only knew.

I have to try to be more present even if it means I have to experience the pain. I think that one of the goals, after the passing of a spouse, is learning how to live with the sorrow.

The question is how do I differentiate between the various emotions and just be with them. I ask myself (I do a lot of that lately), Am I hungry? Sad? Anxious? Sometimes they all feel interchangeable or possibly mixed into one super pain and do I really have to do anything about it? Maybe that's an "aha" moment - to just be. This is a difficult thing for me to do because I am such as an impatient person.

NEW BANKING RULES

I am pretty sure that Frank Spungen was not the first Wells Fargo customer to die, but banks certainly seem to have a lot of problems when customers pass away. I have banked at Wachovia in its many incarnations over the years, and now in its latest name as Wells Fargo. We had both our personal and Frank's business accounts there.

Shortly after I settled into my new apartment, I went to the nearby branch office to officially close out Frank's business account. I was told that there was still $65.00 in the account, I didn't agree with that as I knew that there was no money left in the account. The assistant to the assistant called some special phone number and discussed my issue. The call lasted for about ten minutes during which time, she was frantically scribbling some notes. She then insisted that I be refunded the balance. I never had to be practically forced to take money from a bank before. I should have been more assertive. That should have been my first clue that this transaction was not right. A few weeks later I got a statement from Wells Fargo for the "closed" business line of credit account and there was an interest charge of over $200. I got on the phone and the customer service person spoke to the manager of the bank. I was told to return to the bank with my husband's death certificate and the manager would assist me. The manager immediately turned me over to the same assistant to the assistant. The ATTAs (a new banking acronym that I have created) have a desk, a phone, a computer, and an open office on the banking floor. They are pleasant, but clueless. They feel very powerful, although they know almost nothing about any of the bank's protocols. Whatever issue they need to handle, beyond minor banking business, requires lengthy phone calls to the main corporate office to get instructions on how to handle the subject, and invariably they do it incorrectly. Apparently there was no money in the account, as I told them, but by withdrawing money it triggered account activity and interest started accruing. I insisted, to no avail, that I did not owe the money, but it was told that if I didn't pay the $200 more interest would continue to be applied to the account. All my explanations fell on deaf ears, so I decided to pay the $200 in hopes of making the problem go away. I felt like I was being blackmailed by the bank. Since then I have heard no more about the business account, but I still believe that I was charged in error and that I am owed a refund of $200.

A few weeks later, I called the "800" customer service number to have the bank stop payment on a check from my personal account. The check had been mailed and had never been received. I was told by customer service that I did not have authority to do that. I was a bit perplexed, since we had a joint checking account for fifty years that could be used on an "either or" basis. I thought that meant that either my husband or I could use this account equally. Wrong again! It seems that only one Social Security number and that was my husband's, could control the account. I was getting really upset now.

Eventually my phone call was routed to the Wells Fargo corporate office in California. I was informed that, again, someone with a level of authority would call and speak to the local branch manager and that I should go over to the bank with another death certificate in hand. One more time. What happened was kind of predictable. The manager again referred me to the very same ATTA. If I wasn't so upset, the entire scenario might have been laughable, although really not funny. I looked at the manager and said in a firm, but quiet voice, as I was standing in the middle of the banking floor, "I am going to tell you something and I really don't want you to respond or defend your bank or any of your employees, just listen. I was told that the manager would personally handle this matter and that person is you. I don't ever want the ATTA to ever touch my account or have anything to do with my accounts again. You can do whatever you want with her, but I think that single handedly she could bring Wells Fargo to its knees."

I noticed on future visits to the bank, that the ATTA was still working there, but when she saw me enter the bank, she would get up and scurry away, and hide in the vault. Over time she would stay seated at her desk, but avert her eyes from me.

The manager then took me into his office which was equipped with walls and a door and was designed to give him a higher level of privacy and creditability. He got on the phone and talked for some time, while also scribbling furiously.

226

He told me, "I have to get some new signature cards for you to sign which will make you the primary signatory on the checking account." I asked him why I needed new signature cards since I had signed them 50 years ago. "Why isn't the old card good anymore?" He didn't answer me, maybe the question was too difficult. "I will contact you as soon as I get the paper work. Do you have a death certificate for your husband?"

I expected this so I was prepared and handed over the one that I had brought with me, the third one I had given them in the last month. They had almost cornered the market on Frank Spungen death certificates. Maybe they were planning on papering the walls with Frank Spungen death certificates. "In the meantime, I will stop payment on the check", he added. I almost forgot why I had come into the bank.

This saga goes on. In a few days the manager called.

"I have a new signature card for your checking account and I will mail it to you," he said.

I guess he needed to drag out the process a bit longer. That was also somewhat puzzling as I live less than a mile from the branch office. I think he was afraid for me to come into the bank again and it would be easier to handle me from a distance.

"I need to come over to the bank today to handle some other banking business so I will be in shortly," I said.

When I got there, the manager took me into his office and handed me an 8 ½ x 10 computerized form. Some of the spaces were already filled in with computer generated printing. I sat down at his desk, signed my name, and filled in my Social Security Number under the heading "Primary Checking Account Signatory." Then I noticed about halfway down on the form was a pre-printed entry, "Death Certificate for Frank A. Spungen is on file." When I read the next line, I couldn't believe my eyes. I didn't know if I should laugh or cry. It said "Secondary Signatory, Frank A. Spungen" and his Social Security number. I decided to let it go and see if anyone else noticed it or if this was a new banking regulation to retain deceased customers on their active roles.

A few weeks later, the bank manager called again.

"Would you mind coming in to the branch again to sign another signature card as the previous one was rejected?" he asked.

I went over to the bank and read the form. Frank's name had been removed. I suddenly remembered that some years ago on Saturday Night Live they used to do a faux newscast, the precursor to Jon Stewart and Steven Colbert shows on Comedy Central. There had been a joke about the death of Spain's Generalissimo Franco. It was used in the opening salvo of the comedy news skit. Each week they would announce, "News Flash!" and read some inane headline. One week the news reader said, "Generalissimo Franco of Spain has died."

The joke was that Franco had been deceased for years. It wasn't really news. For the next few months they always opened that portion of the show with, "Generalissimo Franco is still dead." If you enjoyed the humor on SNL, it was really funny.

I handed the newly signed form to the manager, and turned to him. "Frank Spungen is still dead!" I said.

His mouth dropped open and he looked shocked. I didn't have any further incidents with the bank over Frank's accounts or signature. I have used that statement in response to some other similarly ridiculous (from my point of view) problems that have come up, not necessarily related to the banking business. To some people, it may be a bit irreverent, but it always seems to work. At least I know that I had their complete attention. Knowing my late husband's sense of humor, I have a feeling he is chuckling with me over my retort to the bank manager. I realize that I could have switched my checking account to another bank, but I was afraid to do it in case the new bank was even less efficient. Once I got the signature problems handled, which took nearly two months, I thought I should leave my account where it is. Who knows what other issues might arise with a new bank?

I have shared this incident with some other widows and found that they have had similar experiences with banking as well, but they have never mentioned it to others. When we realized the apparent universality of this situation we find it hard to believe how common it is and we all get a good laugh. After sharing some of these bank anecdotes at readings, I have been told by some widowers in my audiences that they did not receive the same treatment from their bank after the death of their wives. In 2012, there was a wonderful English movie starring Judy Dench, among others, titled "The Best Exotic Marigold Hotel." In the opening scene, Judy Dench, playing a recent widow was on the telephone with her bank. It is almost a mirror replay of my experience with the bank. I could tell who the widows were in the audience by who was laughing most heartily at this scene.

BABY STEPS

Two years after Frank's death, after going to the therapist for almost a year, I made plans to visit friends at the seashore, the trip that I couldn't take the year before. I was able to visualize driving over the bridge, not off the bridge. I went with little or no trepidation (Hooray!), but I did get lost which wasn't my fault as I had been given wrong directions by several friends. I drove all over South Jersey, which is not a scenic delight. Fortunately it was day time and the weather was clear. A number of my friends, knowing my fears, kept calling me along the way to check on my progress. My cell phone rang (I do have Bluetooth).

"How are you doing?"

"I am driving on Route 47 South, but it is not familiar to me at all."

"Remember, you haven't been in that area for more than ten years and things change and new stores and homes have been built. Keep driving, you are going in the right direction."

"But it still is totally unfamiliar to me."

Fifteen minutes later, my cell phone rang again. It was different friends, "How are you doing?" they asked.

"I am still on 47 South and the area is still totally unfamiliar to me. In the last ten years I don't think that some higher being built whole towns like Pitman, Franklinville, Millville, and Vineland and just plopped them down, like Lego villages, right there on route 47 South."

But my protestations fell on deaf ears, they didn't believe me. Something was wrong. I decided to look for a gas station to see if I could get some better directions from a real person. I saw a number of gas stations, all boarded up and deserted. They were not just closed because it was Sunday, but they were out of business – this was an economically depressed area, and not considered a main highway anymore as an expressway had been built to parallel the old road. These were all two lane country roads running through a series of small towns. I finally found an open gas station, but the two men who worked there spoke no English, none.

I asked, "Should I turn right or go straight at the next intersection?"

"Straight, right."

I asked again, and he said, "Right, straight."

Confusion reigned in my head as my angst started to increase. I was having a little difficulty conjuring Bill up to assist me. A woman pulled into the gas station and I asked, "Do you speak English and do you know how to get to Wildwood Crest?"

"Yes, and yes," she said and then asked me, "Do you have an iPhone?"

"Yes, I do" I answered.

I also had a GPS in my car and an iPad with me. This was clearly a case of technology overkill. I was so confused by all of them that I forgot I had all these high-tech directional aids and I couldn't find a safe place to pull over to look at them. I longed for my good old paper map of South Jersey that I could never re-fold properly and had to give to my husband to do that. The woman took out her phone, and I took out mine, and she gave me an ad hoc iPhone lesson right there in this old gas station, that only had three pumps and looked as if it were shortly going the way of all the other permanently closed gas stations in this rural area in South Jersey. Melissa (I asked her for her name since she was about to become my new best friend) showed me how to use the Google Maps icon and then she took off. A minute later she turned her car around and pulled up parallel to my car, lowered her window and said, "I don't think you need to deal with this by yourself." I told you that she was my new best friend (at least for the present). I may have looked more upset or stupid than I thought.

"Follow me to the first right turn. I will put my directional blinkers on and wave to you to turn and then I will go straight and be on my way," she said.

In hindsight, I should have gotten her contact information so I could send her a thank you note, but I delivered my thank you on the spot.

"Thanks so much," I said.

"No problem," she responded, "I don't live very far away. She drove out of the gas station and I followed her.

As soon as I made my right turn and got on the proper part of 47 South I knew exactly where I was, my anxiety disappeared, and eventually I got where I was going, albeit, a little late. A two and a half hour ride ended up taking me more than four hours. I wasn't really in a hurry except that my friends had made a dinner reservation at a seafood restaurant in Cape May that specialized in lobster, one of my favorite foods. My mouth was watering for a big steamed lobster and I didn't want to miss that treat. I focused on that lobster dinner and it was smooth sailing after that. I felt like this was a test, maybe set up by my therapist, to see how I would react in such a situation. I think I got a "B" and I was in time for my delicious lobster dinner.

WHO MAKES THE CASSEROLE?

Shortly after I was widowed I noticed that my friendships began to take on a different hue. My husband and I had numerous friends which were usually part of a couple. In addition, I had some girl friends that I had made outside of the couple connection. These included friends from work, school, and a variety of other social activities. I have one friend, Susan, who has been there for me all my life from the day we were born. We lived next door to each other, later just a few streets away, and we were in the same classroom from nursery school through high school and then we were neighbors again. Even our parents were close friends. As we grew up, we may have had different life styles, but we always found our common ground. Both of us experienced the death of a grown child who lived a troubled life and we were instantly there for each other in ways that others were not. This long-term relationship may be somewhat unusual, but not uncommon among women. Women make connections with each other that are long lasting and supportive. They are there to accompany each other for a fun day of shopping or to jump into a help mode when life gets tough. An emotional level often exists in relationships with women that does not compare to bonds between men. This quality differentiates the relationships between men and women and is helpful in allowing the brain to produce a higher level of serotonin which aids in creating a greater feeling of well-being helping to avoid depression. Spending time with girlfriends is good for our health. I think sourcing out new friends is part of the feel good spectrum and we can control the colors.

My husband was a very friendly person but his relationships with other men were of a less supportive nature. Men find common ties in a different way and in a different place than those forged by women. My husband shared time and conversation with other men over sports, politics, hobbies, and lunch clubs, but rarely did he share feelings with the other men in the same way that women do. Frank was quite content to sit by himself doing crossword puzzles, and other solitary word games, which he did in pen, erasable pen was his little secret. He was a wonderful Scrabble player which he turned into a solitary activity by challenging the computer. When he was working he was always playing Scrabble on the computer and the business person on the other end of the phone was none the wiser. After he passed away, I gathered my girlfriends around me like a warm shawl. I was also open to making new friends to help me on my journey. Some couples who had been social friends seemed to pull back and a chasm opened up between us. I don't have too many twosomes that survived. Early on in my grief my doctor informed me that I wasn't to be too surprised if this happened, but I was surprised at this unexpected turn of affairs. After the death of a spouse or partner, friends, specifically girlfriends, often bring the widow a home cooked meal knowing that she has to eat and would most likely prefer to eat her proverbial casserole with friends in the comfort of her own home than in a restaurant. I don't think that I have ever seen a man deliver a home cooked casserole to a grieving widow. The girlfriends might pull up chairs and sit around the dining table or put cushions on the floor, eat the casserole, accompanied by a glass of wine and talk about a myriad of topics. They laugh and cry and share their thoughts. It's amazing to me that seven years ago I didn't know these women. Now, they are some of my best friends. Men may build a small community but it is more solo oriented in nature. Widowers are lonely in a different way than women are and tend to remarry more often and sooner than women.

I have read that the girls will bring you through and they do. The new girlfriends that we discover after age 50 are often different, not better just different, than the friends that we found in our younger years. The new women in our lives fit into our new circumstances. This was not the life that I had planned for, but nonetheless this is where I am. Ranting and raving or pulling the bed covers over my head will not change it. I need to just go with the flow and make the most out of my changed life. It doesn't do any good to compare this life with the old life. I need to make the most of what is unfolding in front of me as I walk through this journey without Frank, but not alone. It is a new learning curve. Sometimes it worked and sometimes it didn't, but I got better at it and my accomplishments started to add up. I did things I was proud of. I participated in activities that I never really thought about doing before and found them enjoyable. Over more than the seven years there were many choices open to me to enjoy with my new girlfriends. I might go out for a meal, or to theater, movies, concerts, museums, classes, meditation group, lectures, meetings, volunteer work, or to book clubs. I tried knitting with a group of friends, but I lost my needles so maybe that was a sign that knitting wasn't for me. Life was being presented to me on a menu and my role was to pick and choose what might be of interest to me. I could take the easy way out and choose not to partake of the many items offered, but life was presenting me with more than that and I needed to take a chance.

I HATE SATURDAYS

The first year after the death of my husband, I never, ever had a good day. I used to look back and think, "Am I feeling better today than I did a week ago? No. Two weeks ago? No. A month ago?" No. The second year was pretty much the same, although I began to have some ray of optimism that tomorrow would be a good day. By the second half of the second year, I started to have what I call "neutral" days. They weren't terrible, but not wonderful either. I began to notice that I'd have some brief moments during the day when I was not focused on my husband's illness and his death, and that was an improvement. I was able to concentrate on other thoughts and activities. I had been told by widows in their whispered words of widowspeak that this would happen, but at the time, I didn't believe them. I thought that they were just trying to make me feel better.

Other noticeable changes can be fewer, such as sleeping better. I don't always jump when the phone rings, I have fewer nightmares. My panic attacks come less often, and I have almost stopped bringing the phone in the bathroom with me in case I have an important call from the doctor or maybe even a call from Frank. I have lost track of how many days and night were spent in emergency rooms and how many admittances there were to various hospitals, some more than once: Southampton Hospital, Stony Brook Hospital, and New York University Hospital. During his hospitalizations Frank would call me early in the morning and ask me, "Are you up, yet? How soon are you coming to the hospital?" No, I wasn't up, yet, but I answered, "I am up. I am just going to take my shower and eat some breakfast and be there as soon as I can." How fast I could get there depended on what hospital he was in at the time.

Now back to good days and bad days. Not all the days in my week are equal. Monday through Friday, I operate on a schedule that keeps getting busier. I go to meetings, doctor appointments, errands, meeting friends for lunch and/or a trip to a museum, or going to the movies, and writing this book. Some parts of days are better or worse than others. Sometimes mornings are good and the afternoons are not so good and vice-a versa. And then there are Saturdays.

Many widows have a dislike for Sundays or the whole weekend because they find that they are more often alone than they are during the weekdays and are without the structure of weekday activities. I personally hate Saturdays the most of all the days and that didn't change significantly the first year or two after Frank's death. Sundays are OK for me. Bottom line is that Sundays are not Saturdays. It also means that I have gotten through Saturday and I have six whole days to go before Saturday comes around again so we can put that on the shelf to deal with until next week. Why do I have such a strong dislike for Saturdays? I have tried swapping out what I do on Saturday with what I do on Sunday. It doesn't work. My Sunday schedule is for relaxing, reading the Sunday newspapers, going to an afternoon movie or watching a sporting event on TV, taking a walk, followed by a nap and that works fine for me.

For many years, I had a history of enjoying Saturday activities with my husband. Out to breakfast or lunch, errands, and food shopping, if the weather was nice, a walk on Long Beach in Sag Harbor, NY and maybe to buy plants for our garden, sometimes an early movie and maybe out to dinner alone or with friends (if we didn't go out to lunch). I didn't realize how ingrained this Saturday schedule was in my life and how much I enjoyed it. It doesn't work very well doing all those things by myself. Saturday seems to be more of a family day with couples, with or without children, seemingly happy, (at least to me) laughing and chatting and often joined by friends, and walking and eating together in groups. I have my list of things to do and go about completing it in a businesslike manner, but my day is joyless and I do it without any emotional pleasure. I feel like I am floating through the day on a cloud unnoticed by others. I am overwhelmed by a pervasive loneliness as I struggle to get through. I am pretty tired by the time I have completed my "to do" list so my next stop is to go home and the day is almost over (no plans for the evening to look forward to-that was then, not so true now). I have survived another Saturday. I try to go to New York to visit my children and grandchildren as often as I can on weekends and I do enjoy the time I spend with my family. I occasionally make plans to go out to dinner or some event on Saturday with friends and that helps some, but the next Saturday comes around and I am back to the beginning. I wish I could petition whoever is in charge of Saturdays and try to get them removed from the calendar.

Now I only suffer through "Sad Saturdays" occasionally. It is possible that I haven't dealt with my sadness that I have accumulated during the week because it gets obscured by my busy schedule and then Saturday comes and I have to face the weekend alone.

FOR WANT OF A HUSBAND

There is a long list of what I missed the most in our relationship after my husband died, and these may differ for each person. Some of the items are pretty self-explanatory and include ordinary every day occurrences like waking up in the morning and seeing my husband sleeping beside me, taking walks, going out for a meal, going to a show or a movie, being a "back seat driver." High on my list is companionship, laughter, and being touched. The other day when the postman in my apartment building handed me my mail, his hand innocently brushed mine – It was an accidental touch, but it sent an electric shock wave though me. I am sorry that I felt it because it made me remember how much I crave the human touch, not necessarily a sexual one, but the intimacy of being touched by someone who cares about you, not just a spouse but other family and friends as well. This includes hugs and kisses, too. There is no substitute for it.

"Will I ever have that again on a regular basis?" I wonder, When I see a couple, walking along holding hands, I never realized how many couples do, my eyes well up with tears for what is missing in my life. "What else do I need a partner for besides touch, and that includes holding hands?" A positive touch is more than an action or a reaction that passes between persons of any gender or age or relationship. When I am with my grandchildren we often hold hands and hug and kiss, it is a beautiful thing for me to experience the warmth and silkiness of their touch. Even though they are old enough to cross any street without holding hands with an adult, I always take their hands when we cross, big or small, because it feels so comforting to me. I think that the lack of human touch makes you want to curl up and die sometimes. It changes your whole outlook on life. For people who live alone, a dog or a cat can be a worthy substitute for the human touch. It is the tactile aspect of a relationship that I miss and yearn for. I am not ready for a pet again as I am allergic to dogs and cats, but not to Guinea pigs or Hamsters. I don't want one of those animals-they are not soft and cuddly enough for me to serve as a companion.

I need a husband to take care of me when I am sick or have a tooth pulled and the list goes on and on, some things big and some things small. One of the items on my long list is that I need my husband to open a bottle of wine. Frank never taught me that skill. I guess he thought he would always be there to do it for me. It took me quite a while to master the art. I tried several different kinds of simple corkscrews, but the corkscrew often went in crooked, not in the center, or the cork went in the bottle. I had the hardest time. If I was successful in finally coaxing the cork out in one piece, my hands and fingers were sore. I thought of pushing the cork into the bottle, but I don't think that counts as the correct way to open a wine bottle.

Eventually I mastered the art and am now fairly successful most of the time. In the beginning I had another related problem; I had a lot of trouble getting the cork separated from the corkscrew once the bottle was opened. After numerous attempts to separate the cork from the corkscrew, and piercing the palm of my hand a few times, in a moment of frustration, I took the corkscrew, with the cork attached, down to the lobby of my apartment building and asked the desk man to disengage it. He looked at me strangely, but did it without any problem or comment. I had considered throwing the corkscrew away with the cork still embedded in it and starting with a new one each time. After all, simple corkscrews are not very expensive—they only cost a few dollars in the supermarket. I was thinking of keeping a fresh supply of new corkscrews on hand and not having to worry about removing the cork. I only occasionally drink a small glass of wine with my dinner, so unless I am having company, it takes me about two weeks to drink a bottle of wine. The total yearly budget for a new corkscrew every time I needed to open a bottle of wine would only be about $100. Not a lot of money, but I thought I should try harder to focus on getting the bottle open myself and learn to remove the cork more easily. I have tried to buy wine with a screw top, but the wine that I want is not always available with the newer tops. A screw top is not always so easy to open, either. You just avoid stabbing yourself in the palm of your hand. I am pleased to say that I am gaining on both parts of the wine opening operation and have not had to throw out any more corkscrews or injure myself. I have gotten pretty quick with the corkscrew; the simpler the mechanism the faster I can open the wine bottle.

Frank and I enjoyed entertaining family and friends a lot – we had dinner parties and barbecues, especially in the summer time. We had a lovely screened eating porch in our Hampton house where we could eat our meals. I tried to eat all of my meals out there. We used to go to the nearby farm markets and buy locally grown veggies and fruit and make simple, but delicious meals. I had a lot of beautiful dishes and platters to serve our dinners. Each item had a back story to it. When I sold my house, I couldn't bear to part with most of those lovely serving items, many of which I had since we were married. I thought I would continue to use them for entertaining in my new home. When I was married, I was the cook and that was a very good arrangement because Frank could not cook anything, but he became the prep chef, chief bottle washer, and sommelier.

Year one went by. Year two went by and I only looked at my pretty dishes and wine glasses, I didn't use them. Finally as I started year three, I did invite two friends for brunch one Sunday. The food was delicious, and I did use some of my nice dishes, but I wasn't very comfortable without Frank by my side and I didn't want to entertain again in the immediate future. I did prove that I could do it. I found it difficult to entertain by myself, part of the enjoyment of having people over for a party was our team of husband and wife. I love home cooked soup, especially vegetable soup made from all the fresh veggies from the farm stands near my home in the Hamptons which Frank would prep for me by peeling, slicing, cutting, and chopping and I would throw it all in the food processor and do the

rest. It is more labor intensive to make the soup by myself and n
nearly as much fun. I miss sharing the tasting part and the lovely
cooking smells wafting through the house. The soup really takes
almost three days from start to finish, about half the time, it is just
simmering on the stove and then gets moved to the refrigerator for
an overnight intermingling of the wonderful flavors. I developed the
recipe (both a vegetarian and meat version) when I was writing the
book about my daughter's life and I christened it "Writers Block
Vegetable Soup." I had started by baking "Writers Block Chocolate
Chip Cookies" but they are so fattening. At least the soup is healthy
and after a few hours of writing and cooking, you have an already
prepared dinner for several nights. I have not yet called it into play
for this book, but then I realize that I should try to cook the soup as a
solo effort. I tried doing it all by myself and it wasn't too difficult,
just more time-consuming, but the fragrant smells wafting through
the apartment were rewarding and welcome and suffused with good
memories.

I like to wear a lot of bracelets and necklaces, but I needed my honey
to take them off and on for me. That is another item I put on my
"Why I need my husband" list. A few years ago, before my husband
passed away, I saw an infomercial on late night TV for some kind of
magnetic apparatus to assist people who live alone with hooking and
unhooking their bracelets and necklaces. I thought, "Why would I
ever need that?" In hindsight, I think that this is a very needed, but
sad, product. I don't know how many in the TV audience ordered the

roduct, but that is a poor substitute for a husband. I had recently been to several craft shows, and I noticed for the first time that many of the beautiful necklaces and bracelets had magnetic clasps which solve that problem and enabling many of us to put our jewelry on by ourselves whether or not we are widowed, divorced, or have arthritis in our hands. The negative to a bracelet made with a magnetic clasp is that the magnets are often so strong that they tend to pick up any metal items that they come close to your wrist. There you are sitting in a restaurant with a fork and knife hanging from your wrist and looking more than a bit foolish.

I have noticed that my long list of "What I couldn't do without a husband to help me" has gotten shorter as time passes as I have learned to do more things by myself and not even give it a second thought. It is a big step in life when you can learn to rely on yourself.

MINING FOR GOLD

I had a very pretty gold and silver jewelry collection which I had bought on trips or received as gifts that my husband had given me for special occasions over the years. They were definitely not high end items encrusted with diamonds and jewels, but simply made. I loved them all. Within the first year after Frank died, the price of gold and silver had risen to new heights. I decided that once I moved into my new apartment I would take an inventory of my jewelry for gold and silver items that I never wear, have no great sentimental value to me, and or were broken, and earrings with no partners. I decided to sell some of the items along with my set of sterling silver flatware that I never really liked, and rarely used, except to polish it.

A friend of mine referred me to a man who bought gold and silver and came to your house to conduct the sale. The jewelry man's pseudonym was Joe "Gold" What other name did you expect? Joe Gold came to my house to look at the pieces that I had considered selling. I was feeling bad about selling some of them and put them back in the drawer. What transpired was like a Fellini movie. I was living in my new apartment, which was not quite finished, but I was not expecting any workman that day, so I thought it was a good time for Joe Gold to come over. That fell apart at 8:00 a.m. when I received several phone calls in a row from the contractors saying that their schedules had changed and they wanted to come over to finish the work. I don't know many people who would turn down such an offer from a contractor. "Who knows when the next time will become available?" I couldn't reschedule Joe Gold as he was already on his way from out of town. I have a 2 bedroom apartment and I was concerned where I would put Joe. By 9:00 a.m. the contractors had all arrived with their helpers making up a work force of four men. They were fixing the carpet and plumbing and rushing back and forth and filling up the apartment with their gear. I stowed Joe in the guest room and shut the door to give him some privacy. There was no available chair in the apartment that we could move into the room so I directed him to sit on the bed. He needed a table and all I had was a small TV tray table. Joe had some safety concerns (his) about all the other people in the apartment as he had a lot of gold jewelry with him from previous customers that he had visited that day. He kept looking more and more nervous about all the traffic and chaos in the apartment. Every time I opened and closed the bedroom door. Joe would ask me in a low voice "Are all those people working in your apartment OK?" Joe was seated on the bed and put out his tools that he needed to verify that the jewelry was solid gold or silver on the TV table. He also had a scale to weigh the metals. He put rubber gloves on. I was not sure exactly what or how he did his job, but it seemed a rather slow and painstaking process and somewhat suspicious looking. At least he didn't have plastic baggies like the drug dealers have on TV shows. He kept calling me to come into the room as he often had questions or wanted to tell me something about one of the pieces. In the meantime, the contractors kept calling me to discuss some of the

250

work they were doing. I noticed as I went in and out of the room some of the workman looked in and had a rather puzzled look on their faces. In the middle of all this action there was a knock on the door and I opened the door to see the building manager standing there with another person. "Deb, would you mind if I showed your apartment to my new assistant?" I replied, "Sure, but the guest room is off limits for now." She looked at me quizzically. Now there were 8 people in the apartment including Joe who was locked in the guest room. Finally after almost 3 hours, Joe Gold was done and gave me a check for what I had sold. He was laughing as he went on his way. The whole morning was really quite entertaining, I did make some money (which I managed to spend on something new I needed for my apartment), and I surely had my laugh for the day.

A TSUNAMI OF GRIEF

I had been through a year of tears, was it really a year or just a moment in time unlike any other years of my life? Too slow, too quick, surreal, unbelievable, unbearable, and there is more to come, much more. Sometimes, I might just forget for a short time--not forget as if the memory disc is wiped clean, but where the thoughts that are uppermost in my mind are suddenly, out of nowhere, washed over by a tsunami of grief and I try to catch my breath and regain my equilibrium. What sets off the tsunami? Is there a trigger? Sometimes it is something simple like seeing other older couples food shopping together or just holding hands. Sometimes it is nothing, and you never know when it is coming. I find that food shopping is especially difficult because we always did it together.

The second spring after Frank's passing I struggled with memories that suddenly flooded back as I pictured my beautiful gardens bursting into bloom. I remembered Frank had put special metal cages on the peony and tomato plants. When Amy, our gardener, saw that he had put them on upside down, she anointed him "Farmer Frank." I felt a deep longing for my home and my tomato plants and cutting gardens. I know that looking back may not be good for you, but it can be quite difficult to stay in the present, or even look to the future. When I would remember certain happy scenarios, Frank was always in them, as he had been in real life, but when I thought of going back, I knew it would never be the same because I would be

alone. Water Mill, New York had been my home for ten years a~
now when I went back I was only a visitor. Living in the Hampton
without Frank was not possible for me and was not something I
wanted to consider. There were other complicating issues which
pretty much constrained me from living there as well. When you
move, under such circumstances, you have to realize that you take
your emotional baggage with you. It doesn't make it all better, but
under certain circumstances, it may help lessen the day-to-day angst.
Frank loved all manner of fresh vegetables and fruit, even the not so
popular ones like lima beans and okra. Now when I see his favorites
items appear in season at the nearby Farmer's Market, I want to buy
them for him and bring them home as a surprise. When I get home,
the surprise is on me because he is not there. I have been tempted to
buy some of this produce and just bring it home as it's good to be
surrounded by sweet memories. He loved okra, which is a funny
vegetable for a Jewish boy from Philadelphia to like as it is more
popular in the south than in the north. I could never find many
recipes to cook okra, other than deep fried or in soups, but whatever
I made, he loved it. I didn't like preparing it. It has a tendency to be
a bit slimy. Last summer, I saw freshly picked okra in little green
baskets at the Pennsylvania Dutch counter at the nearby Farmer's
Market. I got very emotional as my eyes filled with tears and I felt
compelled to put my hand on top of the container for a moment, like
I was channeling him into the okra. In case you are wondering if I
felt embarrassed, none of the other shoppers even noticed my actions
or the tsunami washing over me.

ounds kind of silly, but grief manifests itself in many ways, some not completely rational. There are few early warning signals for the arrival of a tsunami of grief like the system they have in the South Pacific. The tsunami of grief doesn't recede as quickly as it does on the TV news, leaving pain and trauma in its wake. I don't know how to make it go away, there is no clear cut time to how long the after effects will linger. It may hang around for an hour or all day. I think tsunamis come less often now, but they are still there, lurking underwater, making concentric circles as in the upheaval of an earthquake and then wash over me again and again. As the time goes by, weeks, months, and years, the tsunamis may lessen, but I am convinced they will keep coming, unbidden and at some of the most unexpected times.

About two years after Frank died, I went to an event sponsored by Bryn Mawr Graduate School of Social Work which I had attended. I graduated in 1990 and I had lost track of most of my classmates. I was mingling with the others, when I saw and heard the voice of my good friend, Lori, who had been in my class. She had worked for me as well at my agency after her graduation. Over the years, we had both moved out of the immediate area and, as happens with a lot of friendships, we lost contact with each other. Within minutes, we were hugging and kissing each other like high school chums. I call a person like Lori, an "and" friend. No matter how many years we had been out of touch, the first word we both said to each other was "and" and we picked up our conversation where we had last left off.

There were mostly women at this event, so it didn't look odd that was there without my spouse. Lori looked at me, and said, "And how's Frank?" This question was followed by what is called, "A pregnant pause." Frank usually attended these events with me, even if it meant that he was the only man there. He enjoyed meeting my friends and doing whatever I was doing, even being introduced accidentally as "and wife." I guess the look on my face betrayed me before I had a chance to respond. I thought, "What answer should I give her? Maybe, he stayed home to watch the baseball game?"

I blurted out, "Frank passed away two years ago."

That is the kind of answer that can't be sugar coated. It is what it is, unless you can't tell the truth. I saw the look of shock on Lori's face, but she had had no way of knowing what had happened. We hugged some more and exchanged some funny stories about Frank and went on to enjoy the day catching up with our lives.

Later that night after I had gone home, it suddenly hit me what had happened and a tsunami of grief washed over me. I could visualize myself standing, earlier that day on that lovely stone patio on a beautiful sunny day and saying, "Frank passed away two years ago." That sentence was ricocheting around and around in my brain. How did I say those words? I don't know if I whispered them or shouted them, but I said them, and now I regretted uttering them because it suddenly occurred to me that saying those words made them true. I was especially shocked to hear the words, "Two Years." Two years is a very long time. How could it be two years that he was gone when it truly seems like only yesterday?

THE CLOSED SOCIETY

When I am in a room with single women, I almost always can tell which women are widowed and which ones are divorced. Widows seem to have a look of sadness in their eyes and divorced women have a flash of anger in theirs. The widows recognize me as I do them. I think that widowhood is a closed society open to only those who have experienced the death of a husband or partner. Almost nobody talks about what is really happening in mixed company (with people other than widows). When widows know you are a member of their secret society, they incline their head and offer you their condolences in a more public voice and then speak in a very low voice directly into your ear in a secret language called widowspeak:

"It is terrible and painful, but as time goes by (there is that issue of time again that keeps coming up) you will feel a little better, it won't be so overwhelming."

No one can get into the secret society unless her husband has died; the membership is automatic and immediate. The information is downloaded, faster than even American Express gets the data. There is no way to leave or resign; you are forever inscribed on the membership list. Even for widows who have remarried, they still belong.

These same widows will often take me aside and whisper, "I love my husband, but I still miss my first husband. My husband does not really know this. It doesn't really matter how many years have passed." Widowhood leaves a scar on the heart, and for most, the scar does not ever fully heal. The question most commonly asked by other widows is, "How long has it been since your husband has passed away?" Perhaps we are looking for signs of healing, hoping that we, too, might have a chance to move on.

Sometimes I feel that I am imagining that all widows speak the same language to other widows. It is not just what they say, but how they say it. The other night I went to a party with two widows whose husbands had died a few years ago. I had not seen them since Frank had passed away. During the evening, both of them came up to me separately and leaned towards my ear, their hands on my arm or cheek, and said almost identical words to me in widowspeak. I know that I am not imagining the identical words that we all whisper to other widows. They are spoken more as an aside rather than in a tone that others can hear. Now that more time has passed, I have in some cases become the senior widow (in terms of time since my husband's death) in the room. I was recently at a social event and the husband of the hostess, whom I had known for a long time, had passed away a few months ago. I walked up to her and leaned into her ear, as other widows had done to me, and said I was sorry to hear of Gary's death.

She looked up at me and blinked, and whispered in response, "It is terrible isn't it? Does it ever get better?"

I knew that she was speaking volumes to me with just that question. "I am serving food to my guests and I feel so sad. We used to entertain a lot, and here I am doing it by myself. I never imagined that this is what I would be doing in my life."

I have been considering writing a "Widowspeak" dictionary, but I think that it may not be necessary because those outside of the circle have no need for it. We widows intuitively know the words and meanings as soon as they are called into play. I'm not sure if I should tell them the truth,

The second most commonly asked question is, "Do you ever get over it?"

Getting over it should not be a goal because it is unattainable. It is not like a bad head cold. Depending on the circumstances, which are different for each widow, there are levels of "getting over it," but the death becomes indelibly printed on the widow's life like a tattoo that can sometimes be removed, but there are outlines that remain forever inscribed.

After the death, a little door opens and the new words and phrases move in as they suddenly become part of our vocabulary. I have observed that these questions come into play, whether the marriage was a good one or not. They also apply to men who are widowed as well as same sex couples. It pertains more to the severing of the relationship, like the cutting of the umbilical cord because life is never the same after that. The goal is to integrate the loss, not to get over it. These two goals can be unified into your being.

THE TWO WIDOWS

I often feel that I am two widows. I think that I am a sham because there is one of me for public consumption, and the other one is hidden just below the surface. It is not like schizophrenia, but there is a split in me. The hidden one has to be kept under control, which is really not too difficult.

The greeting most people give me either on the phone or face-to-face, "How are you doing today?" is well meaning. I want to respond by saying, "Do you really want to know?" but that might be construed as rude. Sometimes in the early days, I often replied, "I am still here" or "There are no words." I have often thought of having little cards printed up that would offer a variety of brief appropriate answers, at least to me. I could ask the questioner to choose one from the pack and if they didn't like the answer, they could put it back in the stack and take another one. Maybe that would be easier for all concerned.

Then there are some people who really make stupid remarks or ask silly questions, some unwittingly, and I am not sure about the others—maybe they truly don't know what to say. Regardless of the origin of their words, each one is one is like a slap across the face. For instance, "Are you happy you moved back to Philadelphia?" or "Do you miss your home in the Hamptons?" I am often rendered speechless for a moment until I can collect my thoughts and then I feel compelled to respond. I might go babbling on and not say anything profound because what I really want to say is, "What a dumb question." After thinking about it I have come up with a few snappy retorts to keep in my repertoire such as, "How would you feel?" That technique is called answering a question with a question and puts the ball in their court. After a while, it seems better not to try to answer such outrageous questions and nod your head slightly and smile benignly, a variation of the Mona Lisa smile and leave it up to the other person to try and figure it out.

I am sure that everyone who has suffered the death of a loved one has had people say thoughtless things. I think these things are usually not intended to hurt anyone and that it is most likely an inadvertent act on the part of the speaker. They probably want to comfort you, but don't know how and feel that they must say something. No one wants to talk about grief and death, but silence is not comfortable for most people either. I think there is a list of "words that wound" written somewhere. If not there ought to be one that includes all of these insensitive gems. And there are always new ones, often unbelievable utterances, to add to the list. It may be helpful to prepare yourself to respond to these questions or statements by writing down a list of a few comments to have at the ready. It may make you feel better, but keep in mind that it is not the time for a teaching moment.

When I went to Florida the first winter after Frank had passed away, I went to a meeting regarding my possible interest in buying an additional time share. On the sales person's information sheet, it was clearly listed that I was a widow. The rules of time share buyers are unique to time share properties, such as, if you are married, both spouses must attend the sales meeting. I had no intention of buying anything remotely connected to real estate, but they gave me a nice perk for sitting there for 90 minutes and listening to the sales pitch. I got 15,000 Marriott points which would buy me a free night in a Marriott hotel. The salesperson, whose name I don't recall (so Freudian) met me in a small sales room and seated herself across a table from me and asked in a rather brusque manner,

"Where is your husband? Why isn't he here?"

To my left was an empty chair. I guess it was waiting for Frank. I looked at the chair and then to the salesperson and answered, "My husband is where he was last year. He is still dead." Her jaw dropped, but I didn't feel sorry for her because she didn't even take the time to look over my information sheet before speaking to me. I have had occasion to use that sentence a few times in response to some egregious question which stunned me. Obviously I try to save that response for a special occasion and, then, only to make a point that can't be made another way. Most of the time, my goal is not to make the speaker feel uncomfortable; maybe it is to make me feel better. After this little exchange, she began to tell me about her mother's illness and death. I guess she was embarrassed and was trying to build rapport with me and thought I would be a willing listener and an expert in grieving as well. I kept thinking, "This is not about you," and let her go on for a while. When people say insensitive things, for whatever reason, and you call them on it, in their discomfort, they often turn the conversation around and make it about them.

"R" IS FOR RESILIENCE

I believe the most relevant definition of resilience is "bounce back" especially as it refers to widowhood. Some of us are born with a greater level of resilience in life and others have to learn the skills needed. We can obtain these tools through education, through growing up with parents who utilize important resilience tools which we can emulate as children, or we can gain it through psychological counseling to assist us in increasing our ability to become more adept at resilience. There are some people who are not greatly successful in increasing their ability to be more resilient, but it is worthwhile to make the attempt. My mother was widowed three times in her life at the ages of twenty-seven, forty-five, and seventy. I never realized the ramifications of resilience until I was widowed. My mother, who had passed away some years before, became my role model for resilience. When a woman is widowed, the process towards reinventing oneself can be measured by the kind of marriage that the couple shared. I know that the last ten years of our marriage were the best for both of us. Other couples may have experienced a different kind of relationship in their marriage, either positive or negative but that did not mean that their lives hadn't changed after the passing of their spouse. Women who already have a good level of resilience may find that they have an easier time on their journey. In addition to resilience, there are a number of other factors that are called into play. Sometimes there is a feeling of relief after the passing of a husband. Whether attributed to the role of the relationship in the marriage, or the longevity of the marriage, and/or the manner of the death. Sometimes it is a combination of factors. When grief persists, overly long in time and depth, it is often referred to as complicated grief. I think that complicated grief may occur less commonly than previously thought. Yes, many widows are consumed by the loss of their partner which might fall under the heading of complicated grief. There is a universality that all widows bring to the table, but the intensity and depth of grief that a widow experiences is very individual. I brought all of our marriage with me, but especially that wonderful decade as the stepping stone for building a new life. I became a different person than I was before Frank passed away, not better, not worse, just different. Slowly the reinvention of me began to develop. These changes occurred slowly and I can only recognize them in hindsight, but relying on that over used bromide that time heals is probably not helpful.

THE ULTIMATE SUNSET

July 2, 2012 was the second anniversary of Frank's death. The family felt that we needed to be together; just us with no company. Ella was at sleep away camp, but the rest of us, Steve and Suzy, Aliana and David, and Joey were all there. We went to stay together at Suzy and Steve's rental house in Sagaponack, another of the beautiful little villages that make up the Hamptons. It was a lovely summer night and we planned a special dinner and ate outside surrounded by the farm fields burgeoning with crops. We grilled thick steaks, accompanied by two bottles of Frank's favorite red wines. We all gave our personal toasts to Frank. It was a bittersweet night. Right out of a movie setting. The next day just Suzy, Steve and I were together at the house. David and Aliana had gone to the movies. The day had been gray and a little drizzly, and we all felt somewhat incomplete. The memorial dinner was just not enough. We talked about what we might want to do that would fill that hole in our hearts that we were all still feeling.

I suggested that we go over to a place called Long Beach which bordered a beautiful bay that reached all the way to the horizon, and was one of Frank's favorite places to walk and view the sunset. The weather did not promise a sunset for that night, but we decided that was where we wanted to go. We picked armloads of beautiful wild flowers which were growing at the rental house and drove over to Long Beach. We divided the flowers into 4 huge bouquets and we each took one and walked to the water's edge, small lapping waves washing the shore line, the sky still gray and overcast. One after the other, we threw our bouquets into the water. Suddenly a small area of the gray sky opened up and revealed a beautiful blue patch. As we continued to stand there, the patch quickly increased in size and within minutes there was one of the most beautiful sunsets I have ever seen at Long Beach. We stared in wonderment and awe. Did Frank have something to do with that beautiful display of nature? I don't know, but we all believed he was there with us and staged that sunset and that he would be with us forever. And now I can get on with my life.

EPILOGUE
FINDING MY VOICE

We all have a voice deep inside of us, but often we are not able to find it. Sometimes it has to be freed and allowed to bubble up. After the almost two year hiatus when I didn't work on the book, my editor gave me an assignment. "Don't write, read." I was to read the 95 pages I had already written. I sat down on a comfortable chair and put the pile of computer written pages on my lap and thought, "Well, here goes." I read most of the manuscript out loud as if I were presenting it to an audience; an audience of one. The more I read, the more engrossed I became. I heard my voice begin to awaken with the realization that these were truly my words and my emotions. I had been able to recapture in the book what I had been feeling. I felt a visceral response rise up in a very powerful way. I was about halfway through the manuscript when I realized that I had to pause to catch my breath. I was in that dual space where I didn't want to stop reading and at the same time I had to take a break to let it wash over me. I was surprised. This was my life I was reading about and I had such a strong reaction to the loneliness and isolation I had gone through. In a few minutes I was able to able to return to reading the manuscript. I did not put it aside or cry. In fact, I was feeling better now. I was coming out on the other side. I had conquered my fears in hearing my voice telling my story. That was a big moment for me. I felt like I was making progress, I was not stuck in the past. Writing for me was the key to my new life. It gave me the gift to living my life in the present and not in the past. After I read the first 95 pages I took some time to process what I had learned about my journey. Some things I had forgotten, some things were as if they had just happened yesterday, and some were memories that had been dormant and now reappeared with great clarity. I was not sad to be able to have them back into my consciousness. During the first few months of my widowhood one of the memories that I had treasured and welcomed back was a little scenario that I played out whenever I went out of my house to do items such as food shopping or a doctor's appointments. When I returned home, to an empty house, my eyes filled with tears. I made up a few little songs about Frank and sang them out loud (and I can't carry a tune, but that didn't matter). By the time I finished my impromptu concert, I would be feeling much better. One day I noticed that I came in the door without singing one of my songs. After another few weeks I found that I didn't need the songs any longer to give me the strength to come in without Frank being there to welcome me. But I seem to have forgotten the words to the two or three songs that I had made up. Maybe someday they will come back to me, but in the meantime it gave me happiness to remember that I was making progress.

When I first began to write my story I was enveloped by sadness as I ate at my table for one. Similar to forgetting the words to the song, the pain of being alone at home or in a restaurant began to subside. Slowly, the feeling receded without much effort by me. Life began to change and it didn't matter if I was alone at the table as my journey unfolded.

These days I even enjoy a solitary meal, at my table for one...

About the Author

Born in Philadelphia, Deborah Spungen graduated from the University of Pennsylvania in 1958. She married Frank Spungen in 1956.

She founded the Philadelphia nonprofit Families of Murder Victims (FMV) and served as its Executive Director from 1985 to 1993. In 1991 she helped develop and introduce the Student Anti-Violence Education Program (SAVE). She assisted in the development of an umbrella organization, the Anti-Violence Partnership of Philadelphia (AVP) which was formed in 1991. She still serves on the board.

Spungen received her Master of Social Service and Master of Law and Social Policy from Bryn Mawr School of Social Service in 1989.

She is the author of *"And I Don't Want to Live This Life"* and a textbook *"Homicide: The Hidden Victims."*

Deborah belongs to an organization called The Transition Network (TTN) which is for women over 50 who are in transition and enjoys their many activities. Her interests include movies, reading and cooking.

She is the proud grandmother of Ella and Joey.

CPSIA information can be obtained
at www.ICGtesting.com
Printed in the USA
LVHW09s2350181018
594105LV00001B/90/P